"Andrew Fuller was an able Baptist pastor who served at Kettering in Northamptonshire from 1782 down to his death in 1815. He was also a theologian who, more than any other, was responsible for persuading most Baptists not to leave the conversion of men and women to the Almighty but to proclaim that it is the duty of sinners to believe in Christ. From its foundation in 1792 Fuller acted as secretary of the Baptist Missionary Society that, under the leadership of William Carey, was spreading the gospel in India. Fuller wanted Christopher Anderson, a young pastor in Edinburgh, to succeed him in his Kettering church and in the BMS work. This carefully annotated edition of their correspondence, containing frank discussion of theological questions, missionary issues and personal troubles, shows something of the practical spiritual life of two dedicated ministers of the gospel."

David Bebbington
Emeritus Professor of History,
University of Stirling.

"Andrew Fuller's close friendship with and mentoring of Christopher Anderson is something that I have long desired to see fleshed out in book form. And thus I am positively elated to see this fresh study of their relationship as well as what remains of their correspondence. This is further proof of Fuller's ability to develop and maintain deep friendships. Moreover, it also serves to remind us of the important ministry of Christopher Anderson, who was such a vital figure in the history of Baptist witness in Scotland. A gem!"

Michael A.G. Haykin
Chair & Professor of Church History,
The Southern Baptist Theological Seminary

"This sweet, brief collection of correspondence between Andrew Fuller and his younger friend, Christopher Anderson, shows something of a spiritual father-son relationship wrapped in a spirit of cordial fraternity. While many crave a kind of formal 'mentoring,' this shows the reality at its natural and tender best. Here is a refreshing mutuality of respect, affection, sympathy, concern, humility, and the pursuit of God's glory. Unspectacular, and yet with something of heaven's gleam about the friendship, this is a soothing, satisfying, stimulating book that will encourage the hearts of God's servants who read it."

Jeremy Walker
Author, *On the Side of God: The Life and Labors of Andrew*;
Pastor, Maidenbower Baptist Church

"Andrew Fuller's influential ministry made profound contributions in theology, missiology, and apologetics, but what draws me to Fuller's life and writings is that he addressed all topics with the sober-minded clarity of a working pastor. Fuller was, above all else, a gospel shepherd. As a gospel shepherd, Fuller knew the importance of and spent time nurturing Christian friendships. This volume, *Under the Mulberry Tree: The Correspondence of Andrew Fuller and Christopher Anderson*, provides a beautiful example of Fuller nurturing a Christian friendship with a fellow gospel shepherd. Clearly, Fuller is the mentor in the relationship, but his letters to Anderson are not in the least transactional but lovingly relational as brothers seek to walk together through daily life with Jesus."

David E. Prince
Assistant Professor of Christian Preaching, The Southern Baptist Theological Seminary; Author, *Preaching the Truth as it is in Jesus: A Reader on Andrew Fuller*

under the mulberry tree

The correspondence of
Andrew Fuller & Christopher Anderson

Brian Talbot and Chance Faulkner

Under the Mulberry Tree

Copyright © 2023 Brian Talbot and Chance Faulkner
All rights reserved. This book may not be reproduced, in whole or in part, without written permission from the publishers.

H&E Publishing, West Lorne, Ontario
www.hesedandemet.com

Cover and layout design by Chance Faulkner

Paperback ISBN: 978-1-77484-116-7
eBook ISBN: 978-1-77484-117-4

Contents

Who Was Christopher Anderson?...1

1806
1. Anderson to Fuller
   [1806?]..17

1807
2. Anderson to Fuller
   August 18, 1807...19
3. Fuller to Anderson
   September 1, 1807...23
4. Anderson to Fuller
   November 1807..25

1808
5. Fuller to Anderson
   February 16, 1808 27
6. Anderson to Fuller
   July 1, 1808 31

1809
7. Fuller to Anderson
   February 21, 1809..33
8. Fuller to Anderson
   May 1809...35
9. Anderson to Fuller
   June 30, 1809 37

10. Anderson to Fuller
   August 18, 1809 39
11. Fuller to Anderson
   August 22, 1809 43

1810

12. Anderson to Fuller
   April 22, 1810 47
13. Fuller to Anderson
   May 17, 1810 49

1811

14. Fuller to Anderson
   May 17, 1811 51
15. Fuller to Anderson
   December 4, 1811 53
16. Anderson to Fuller
   December 10, 1811 57
17. Fuller to Anderson
   December 31, 1811 59

1812

18. Anderson to Fuller
   February 1812 63
19. Fuller to Anderson
   May 4, 1812 67
20. Anderson to Fuller
   May 23, 1812 71
21. Anderson to Fuller
   June 22, 1812 75

22. Fuller to Anderson
   July 2, 1812 79
23. Anderson to Fuller
   September 23, 1812 81
24. Fuller to Anderson
   September 27, 1812 83

1813

25. Anderson to Fuller
   February 6, 1813 87
26. Fuller to Anderson
   February 21, 1813 89
27. Anderson to Fuller
   February 27, 1813 91
28. Anderson to Fuller
   April 2, 1813 93
29. Fuller to Anderson
   May 25, 1813 97
30. Anderson to Fuller
   June 9, 1813 99
31 Fuller to Anderson
   June 14, 1813 101
32. Anderson to Fuller
   December 1, 1813 103
33. Anderson to Fuller
   December 1, 1813 105

1814

34. Anderson to Fuller
    July 7, 1814 107

35. Fuller to Anderson
    October 1, 1814 109

36. Fuller to Anderson
    December 22, 1814 111

37. Anderson to Fuller
    December 29, 1814 113

1815

38. Fuller to Anderson
    January 2, 1815 115

39. Fuller to Anderson
    February 18, 1815 117

40. Anderson to Fuller
    March 10, 1815 119

Appendix

1. Anderson to Ryland (On the death of Fuller)
    May 9, 1815 121
2. Anderson on Fuller 123
3. Fuller to Ward 125
4. Fuller to Marshman 127
5. Fuller to Ward 129
6. Fuller to Ward 133
7. Satchell to Anderson 135

Index 137

Chronology of Christopher Anderson

1782	February 19—Born in Edinburgh, Scotland
1796	Apprenticed as Iron Monger to John Muir
1799	July—conversion
	October 11, Meets Andrew Fuller
1801	October—desire to be a missionary first made known
1802	Meeting with Fuller
1804	December—Death of Anderson's father, William
1805	June—Left Edinburgh for England
	October—Left Olney for Bristol
1806	August 18—Returned to Edinburgh, Scotland
1808	January 21—Ordination
1816	Marriage to Esther Athill
1818	Church enlarged and relocated to Charlotte Chapel
1823	Death of child
1824	Death of wife Esther
1825	Death of two daughters
1826	Death of son Christopher
1828	Death of last-child, William
1851	July—Anderson is removed from the church
	September 5—Death of Mrs. William Anderson
1852	February 18—Death

Who Was Christopher Anderson?

Chance Faulkner

Christopher Anderson (1782-1852) was born in Edinburgh, Scotland, on February 19, 1782, to godly congregationalist parents William Anderson (1744-1804) and Jean Moubray.[1]

Although Anderson was raised in a believing home he was determined to experience the enjoyments of the world in as far as could be permitted without the appearance of contradicting the godly family in which he was raised.[2] It was through the preaching of James Haldane (1768-1851) of the Tabernacle that Anderson received "the strongest impression" on his mind "if not the direct means of his conversion."[3] The Tabernacle is where he first gave "eternal thanks to my dear Redeemer, who has recalled me from my former stupidity, and made me see the riches of His grace, His will and power to save, as well as ... my hardness of heart and rebellion against the kindness of the Saviour, and the most loving Lord."[4] He was baptized as a believer in March 1800.

Three months after his conversion, Andrew Fuller (1754-1815) arrived in Edinburgh on October 11, 1799, to raise support for the Baptist Missionary Society,[5] and left such an im-

---

[1] Hugh Anderson, *The Life and Letters of Christopher Anderson* (Edinburgh: William P. Kennedy/London: Hamilton Adams, and Co., n.d), 3.
[2] Anderson, *Life and Letters*, 6.
[3] Anderson, *Life and Letters*, 7.
[4] Anderson, *Life and Letters*, 9.
[5] Fuller was surprised by the generous support of the Scottish churches. His biographer writes: "To no class of Christians is the mission more indebted, than to our Scottish brethren, whose liberality not only essentially contributed to its prosperity, and gave a powerful stimulus to the activities of its principal agent, but whose multi-

pression on Anderson that "the work of the ministry among the heathen began to rise in his mind."[6] Fuller's second visit occurred in September 1802, where Fuller "encouraged him to cherish the hope of being engaged in the work of the mission." He was accepted immediately by the Baptist Missionary Society. On May 17, 1805, at the age of twenty-three, Anderson sailed to London and was taken under the tutelage of John Sutcliff (1752–1814) of Olney.[7]

By September 1805, Anderson came under the conviction that it was not the "will of Providence" for him to be a missionary to India as he originally planned and desired.[8] Instead he returned to Edinburgh to establish a church "in conformity with the ideas of a New Testament church."[9] The reason for this decision not to be a missionary was twofold: the first was that his constitution would not stand the warm climate of India, and the second was that Fuller desired him to stay home for his usefulness.[10] Additionally, a group of Edinburgh Baptists' "thoughts [were] turned towards Christopher Anderson as their future pastor."[11]

Anderson was officially called by the church at Richmond Court to be their pastor and ordained on January 21, 1808.[12] Richmond Court was the first English Baptist church in Edin-

---

plied kindnesses made a deep and lasting impression on the heart of the Secretary." (J.W. Morris, *Memoirs of the Life and Writings of the Rev. Andrew Fuller* [Boston: Lincoln & Edmands, 1830], 94).

[6] Anderson, *Life and Letters*, 19.
[7] Anderson, *Life and Letters*, 31.
[8] Anderson, *Life and Letters*, 43.
[9] Anderson, *Life and Letters*, 43.
[10] Anderson, *Life and Letters*, 418. The Baptist Missionary Society thought that it was best he stayed home in support of the Society, and his usefulness was needed back in England and Scotland. This is a similar reason that Samuel Pearce did not go to India (Andrew Fuller, *The Life of Samuel Pearce* [Peterborough, ON: H&E Publishing, 2020], 34–35).
[11] Anderson, *Life and Letters*, 63.
[12] Anderson, *Life and Letters*, 79, 82.

Who Was Christopher Anderson?

burgh. For many years the meeting place, which could hold three hundred, was so well attended that they had to turn people away.[13] In 1818 a suitable place of worship was found in Charlotte Chapel.[14] This new building could seat seven to eight hundred and was soon also filled with hearers.[15]

Anderson was convinced that foreign mission was not his calling. However, his desire to reach the lost was not quenched, and so he focused his evangelistic efforts at home in Scotland.[16] As a result, sometime around 1808, Anderson sought with George Barclay (1774–1838) to form an association supporting itinerant preachers in the Highlands. In August and September 1808, he did a preaching tour through Ireland, and a second in 1810.

Andrew Fuller's support of Anderson continued throughout his ministry. Fuller wanted Anderson to replace him as pastor of Kettering and secretary of the BMS. Although this was not to be, Anderson was a founder and secretary of the Edinburgh Bible Society[17] and formed the Gaelic School Society for promoting education in the Highlands.

Among the books he published, two were especially significant: *Memorial on behalf of the Native Irish, with a view on their improvement in moral and religious knowledge through the medium of their own language* (1815); and *Memorial respecting the diffusion of the Scriptures, throughout the United Kingdom particularly in the Celtic or Iberian Dialect*s (1819) a groundbreaking book which led to the Irish Society and the forming of many schools in Ireland for the sake of the literacy of the

---

[13] Anderson, *Life and Letters*, 96.
[14] Anderson, *Life and Letters*, 98.
[15] Anderson, *Life and Letters*, 367.
[16] Anderson, *Life and Letters*, 99, 101.
[17] Anderson, *Life and Letters*, 116

nation.[18] For many of the people in the Scottish Highlands were illiterate. The reform of literacy in Ireland was a direct result of his publications.

The years 1823–1828 were a time of severe domestic trial. In five years, Anderson lost his entire household—his wife and four children.[19] Yet he did not despair, and for the next twenty years faithfully pastored his church. Using his sorrows alongside the full counsel of God, he was able to minister tenderly to those who had experienced loss and point them to the "infinite love of God."[20] On February 18, 1852, Anderson's faith became sight and he "'reaped life everlasting' through Him whose name is love."[21]

The Correspondence of Fuller and Anderson

We have available for us today forty letters of correspondence exchanged over eight years. Although Fuller and Anderson first met in 1802, their letters of correspondence, available in Anderson's biography, date from 1807–1815—the first of the letters of Fuller is likely in 1806, and the last from Anderson is dated March 10, 1815.

Fuller's correspondence with Anderson provides a helpful example of what it looks like for an older, more experienced minister to mentor someone early in his ministry. Although Fuller was older in the faith—twenty-eight years older—and it is evident that Anderson looked to him for guidance and wisdom as a mentor, there is still a shared friendship and mutual respect. Fuller treats Anderson as a co-labourer and friend. Much of the content of these letters has to do with

---

[18] Anderson, *Life and Letters*, 140–146.
[19] Anderson, *Life and Letters*, 171–173.
[20] Anderson, *Life and Letters*, 394.
[21] Anderson, *Life and Letters*, 143.

providing updates on their everyday lives: everything from travel plans, ministry updates, the state of their souls, news of other ministers, Scripture verses, what they are reading and thinking about, and business updates regarding the ministries they were partnered in (Baptist Missionary Society, the Bible Society, the *Baptist Magazine*, etc.). They also shared their fears, struggles, and hardships, and gave one another warnings, encouragement, and counsel. There are a few particular things that stand out.

"I long very much ... to be with you"
One of the first notable observations apparent in their correspondence is that they long to converse and eagerly anticipate letters from one another. However, they realize that while letters are helpful, they are not the ideal or preferred situation. Ultimately, they desire to be personally present in each other's lives and to speak face-to-face. Anderson repeatedly communicates his desire to meet with Fuller on at least six different instances.[22] He longs to see his older mentor: someone he looks up to, can enjoy godly conversation with, plan and brainstorm ministry usefulness, pour out his struggles to, and have personal communion with: "I long very much occasionally to be with you."[23]

Anderson was "glad" to receive letters from Fuller, desiring to hear his counsel and wisdom, telling Fuller, "I shall feel somewhat anxious till I hear from you."[24] Anderson remembers fond times of sitting with Fuller under a mulberry—

---

[22] Anderson, *Life and Letters*, 185, 200, 203, 206 (x2), 225. Fuller visited Scotland at least five times: 1799, 1802, 1805, 1808, and 1813. John Ryland, *The Work of Faith, the Labour of Love, and the Patience of Hope, illustrated; in the Life and Death of the Rev. Andrew Fuller*, 2nd ed. (London: Button & Son, 1818), 156.

[23] Anderson to Fuller, February 1812, in Anderson, *Life and Letters*, 200.

[24] Anderson to Fuller, August 18, 1807, in Anderson, *Life and Letters*, 77

likely a tree somewhere near Fuller's property—when he was in England, receiving his advice, pouring out his heart, and sharing in godly conversation. "I thank you, my dear friend, for your 'Letters.' They are to me sweet."[25]

Undoubtedly, letters are limited to what one can express in words, and thus conversation is limited, since one has to wait for replies. In face-to-face conversation, much more can be communicated in a shorter time, and the company is more enjoyable. Collaboration is more straightforward, allowing ideas to be bounced back and forth. There are important issues that only in-person correspondence can resolve.

One pressing issue we see in the letters is the need to find an assistant to help Fuller with the Baptist Missionary Society. Anderson says:

> Matters appear, in your own apprehension, to be in such a state as to call for some speedy arrangement, and when I saw the note in the *Evangelical Magazine*, advertising your preaching in June, I wished occasionally, for the sake of the Mission and my own soul, that I could be with you, to pray and ponder over the path of duty.[26]

Not only would it be beneficial for the sake of the Missionary Society, but "for the sake of ... my [Anderson's] soul." Anderson expresses this in his own words: "It is nothing short of my coming to see you, or of our meeting together somewhere, if the Lord will. Many things I could then state which cannot be communicated, or at least settled by epistolary correspondence."[27] Unfortunately, Fuller was 400 miles from Ed-

---

[25] Anderson to Fuller, April 22, 1810 in Anderson, *Life and Letters*, 190–191.
[26] Anderson to Fuller, May 23, 1812, in Anderson, *Life and Letters*, 202–204.
[27] Anderson to Fuller, June 22, 1812, in Anderson, *Life and Letters*, 206.

Who Was Christopher Anderson?

inburgh, and finding a place they could both meet would be a sacrifice to both parties. Even 200 miles would take several days to travel.[28]

Fuller writes to Anderson on July 2, 1812, saying, "I wish to see you," and if Anderson can make the trip, Fuller will be at Derby, almost three hundred miles from Edinburgh. Fuller requests Anderson to "reach that place by Wednesday [July 15]."[29]

On the death of Sutcliff, Anderson longed to be with Fuller and to spend as long as he could with him, and committed to making the trip:

> Since I came to Liverpool and have heard this [death of Sutcliff], I am the more anxious to see you. I feel to yourself differently from what I did before. On Monday I shall leave this to meet with you, and shall remain as long as I can, consistently with my engagement to be at Edinburgh by Lord's-day. Yours very affectionately.[30]

Michael Haykin rightly summarizes the importance of face-to-face encounters: "The face-to-face image implies a conversation, a sharing of confidences and consequently a meeting of minds, goals, and direction. One of the benefits of face-to-face encounters between friends is the heightened insight that such encounters produce."[31] These encounters

---

[28] The average journey speed on the poorly maintained roads in England was approximately seven miles per hour. See Dan Bogart, "Turnpike Trusts and the Transportation Revolution in 18th Century England," Figure 2: Average Journey Miles Per-Hour, 1750-1829, [37]. https://www.economics.uci.edu/files/docs/workingpapers/2004-05/Bogart-02.pdf (Accessed August 27, 2023).
[29] Fuller to Anderson, July 2, 1812, in Anderson, *Life and Letters*, 206-207.
[30] Anderson to Fuller, July 7, 1812, in Anderson, *Life and Letters*, 225.
[31] Michael A.G. Haykin, *Eight Women of Faith* (Wheaton, IL: Crossway, 2016), 95.

were undoubtedly true for Anderson and Fuller. When believers are separated from being face to face, it produces a longing in which only the future enjoyment of heaven can abate. Anderson says to Fuller:

> I long very much occasionally to be with you. The Redeemer prepares completely the mansions of His people; but it is not inconsistent with love to Him, that the departure of His children should render heaven more desirable, and, in a subordinate sense, prepare their way. I am sure if you should go before me, I shall include you in my ideas of future enjoyment, as I now do the names of [Samuel] Pearce and others. [32]

One aspect of the future enjoyment of heaven is being reunited with friends whom we were separated from on earth by circumstances, distance, or death. Even though there are limits to personal communion in the present age, the future hope of heaven comforts Anderson.

"*My beloved Father in Christ Jesus*"

Anderson's language towards Fuller was frequently one of deep affection. Most of their letters begin with the familial term "dear brother,"[33] with an endearing adjective added: "my very dear brother;"[34] "I am, my dear brother, yours with inviolable and unfading affection;"[35] "I am dear brother, affectionately yours;"[36] "I am ever, with esteem, yours un-

---

[32] Anderson to Fuller, February 1812, in Anderson, *Life and Letters*, 200.
[33] Anderson, *Life* and Letters, 77, 183, 185, 160, 190, 200, 202, 206, 215, 219, 226, 228.
[34] Anderson, *Life and Letters*, 185.
[35] Anderson, *Life and Letters*, 214.
[36] Anderson, *Life and Letters*, 215.

Who Was Christopher Anderson?

feignedly;"[37] "I am ever, with highest esteem and affection."[38] "Excuse this hurried scrawl I intended to merely show that it is in my heart to live and die with you."[39]

Anderson also addresses Fuller as "my beloved Father in Christ Jesus,"[40] in one of his last letters, saying, "certainly I do feel towards you no small degree of tenderness and sympathy of a child."[41] By the end of Fuller's life, and years of correspondence, Anderson saw Fuller not only as just a co-worker but as a father. There is a temptation for young men to move beyond the point of desiring wisdom from those older than they are, and to take their friendships for granted. It would have been easy for Anderson to see Fuller as a friend, or co-laborer, and not see his need for Fuller as the mentor that he was. Yet this is not so with Anderson; up until their last letters, it is evident that Anderson saw him as a father in the faith. He didn't view Fuller as a life-coach whom he could gain life-hacks from, but as a father to "live and die" with.

Struggles and advice

Their correspondence also shows the freedom to confess their struggles and difficulties. In August 1807, Anderson was not sure what his next steps were in Edinburgh. He writes:

> I find my situation in some respects peculiar and difficult. ... I have no person as yet whom I can call a right-hand man, nor have I had one all along who could enter

---

[37] Anderson, *Life and Letters*, 219.
[38] Anderson, *Life and Letters*, 230.
[39] Anderson, *Life and Letters*, 211.
[40] Anderson, *Life and Letters*, 226.
[41] Anderson, *Life and Letters*, 226.

into my difficulties. But I can unbosom[42] myself to you, and your advice, I know, will not be withheld.[43]

Anderson had enough savings to support himself while preaching, but no official church had begun, and his money was running out.[44] Fuller's response was fatherly. He empathized with Anderson's dilemma and mentioned that the same things have been on his mind on behalf of Anderson. Fuller admits that "I am at a loss as to advising you on the question."[45] Fuller was not willing to give advice when he was unsure, but instead shared his own similar experiences.

Fuller was not unaware of his influence on Anderson's life. In a letter to William Ward, he admits his desire to bring Anderson back to England: "If I dare try to remove him from Edinburgh, and could induce him to come and be co-pastor with me, I would divide my income with him; and he would take my place in the Mission, if he survived me."[46] Fuller wanted Anderson to co-pastor with him and replace him as the secretary of the Baptist Missionary Society. But it is after Anderson made up his mind and called to be a pastor that Fuller tells him his heart: "I dared not mention while your mind was undecided," says Fuller, "... But now, it seems, my hopes are at an end."[47] Fuller could likely have easily persuaded his young friend to come to England so that they might do ministry together. But Fuller wanted Anderson to make up his own mind regarding his work in Edinburgh before he made the offer.

---

[42] Unburden.
[43] Anderson, *Life and Letters*, 75.
[44] Anderson, *Life and Letters*, 75–77.
[45] Anderson, *Life and Letters*, 77.
[46] Fuller to Ward, December 10, 1807 in Anderson, *Life and Letters*, 182.
[47] Anderson, *Life and Letters*, 183.

Who Was Christopher Anderson?

On the death of Anderson's nine-year-old niece, Jeannie, he writes to inform Fuller and ask for encouragement: "I am writing to a beloved brother, who, I know well, has drunk deep in the cup of trial."[48] Fuller is genuinely sympathetic. At this time, Fuller himself had lost fourteen of his children and a wife: "I have lost an affectionate wife and fourteen children. The heaviest loss among the children," according to Fuller, "was a little girl between six and seven."[49] This note is enlightening for a couple of reasons: first, Fuller tells Anderson something extremely personal that is not even documented anywhere else. Fuller had seventeen children, eleven of which died before adulthood.[50] Fuller's count of fourteen children possibly suggests that his wives had three miscarriages.[51] Not only does this show Fuller's willingness to share such personal information, but it also provides a better understanding of the fact that Fuller had indeed "drunk deep in the cup of trial."

Fuller points Anderson to two texts which had brought comfort to his own life during his afflictions: Leviticus 9–10, and Jeremiah 4. He concludes his letter by reminding Anderson that God uses trials in the lives of Christians to bring forth fruit and to show "the reality of your faith, and the efficacy of your hope."[52] Anderson would eventually experience a more severe domestic trial at the loss of his entire household, his wife and children, and would go on to live for another thirty

---

[48] Anderson, *Life and Letters*, 159.
[49] Anderson, *Life and Letters*, 160-162.
[50] Fuller and Sarah Gardiner (1756-1792), his first wife, had eleven children and eight didn't reach adulthood. His second wife, Ann Coles (d. 1825), had six children and three didn't reach adulthood. See Matthew Haste, "Marriage and Family in the Life of Andrew Fuller," *Southern Baptist Journal of Theology* 17.1 (2013): 29, 31.
[51] For more on Fuller and Family see Matthew Haste, "Marriage and Family in the Life of Andrew Fuller," *Southern Baptist Journal of Theology* 17.1 (2013): 28-34.
[52] Anderson, *Life and Letters*, 162.

years. Though Fuller was not alive during this tragic period in Anderson's life, it is quite possible Anderson received much encouragement through this same letter from Fuller written many years earlier. Anderson himself would go on to comfort others in his congregation who would have similar trials.[53] Fuller knew first-hand that "the greatest qualifications, the best instruction, the most useful learning, that any Christian minister can obtain, without any disparagement of other kinds of learning, is that which is attained in the school of affliction; it is by this that he becomes able to feel, to sympathize, and to speak a word in season to them that are weary."[54]

Fuller does not refrain from talking about his personal life, his health, and his struggles.[55] Some of his letters were written in the form of a diary as a means of providing an update on his life.[56] Part of being a mentor means sharing real life with those who are looking to us. By sharing his real struggles, he is not giving Anderson a false expectation of what life looks like as an older man in the faith, and provides trust and intimacy.

Because of the intimate relationship Fuller had with Anderson, he did not have to be shy of providing warnings to his younger friend.[57] In his very last letter to Anderson, the dying Fuller was concerned with a point of doctrine. Thinking Anderson to be in doubt on the point of the doctrine of the perseverance of the saints, he was willing to confront him: "if

---

[53] See Anderson to Mrs. Storrar, October 26, 1826 in Anderson, *Life and* Letters, 392-393; Anderson to Hugh Anderson, August 5, 1849 in Anderson, *Life and* Letters, 393-395; Anderson to Hugh Anderson, Augusts 19, 1849 in Anderson, *Life and Letters*, 395-396.

[54] Andrew Fuller, "Sermon XXXIII: All Things Working Together For Good" in *The Complete Works of Andrew Fuller*, ed. Andrew Gunton Fuller, 3 vols. (reprint; Harrisonburg, VA: Sprinkle Publications, 1988), 1:391.

[55] Anderson, *Life and Letters*, 192-193, 200-202, 219-220, 226.

[56] Anderson, *Life and Letters*, 198, 211-212.

[57] Anderson, *Life and Letters*, 215-216.

Who Was Christopher Anderson?

believers may apostatize and be lost, a consciousness of being a believer would afford no such evidence. ... Let me hear from you, and tell me your mind on this subject."[58] This concern proved to be unwarranted, for Anderson assured him that his fears "are groundless. ... God is possessed of infinite wisdom to devise the plan of redemption, His grace and power are equal to carry to execution."[59] Anderson too at times is not shy to provide advice[60] or critique to Fuller.[61]

Practical matters
Along with the many things they discuss in their correspondence, a majority of it seems to be practical matters. Fuller and Anderson shared much of their life, even if not face-to-face, and their ministries were very much intertwined. They often provided updates on their ministry and projects—whether that be Anderson's ministry to the Irish,[62] Fuller and the Bible Society[63]—the *Periodical Accounts*,[64] what they were reading,[65] the Baptist Missionary Society,[66] or the *Baptist Magazine*.[67] This area, though it might seem insignificant or dull, deserves our attention.

Their relationship and friendship grew in the context of shared interests and doing life together. Both were ministers of the gospel, were part of the Baptist Missionary Society, desired the salvation of the lost, and cared deeply about being

---

[58] Anderson, *Life and Letters*, 229.
[59] Anderson, *Life and Letters*, 229.
[60] Anderson, *Life and Letters*, 205–206, 216–218.
[61] Anderson, *Life and Letters*, 214.
[62] Anderson, *Life and Letters*, 185.
[63] Anderson, *Life and Letters*, 187, 190–191, 192.
[64] Anderson, *Life and Letters*, 189, 190.
[65] Anderson, *Life and Letters*, 189.
[66] Anderson, *Life and Letters*, 190, 193.
[67] Anderson, *Life and Letters*, 187–188, 195–196.

men of usefulness for the kingdom of Christ and the good of others. Discipleship is not simply a scheduled program; it happens in the context of intentionally doing life together.

Investing in the future

Fuller was certainly intentional in his discipleship. Looking to the future he desired to raise other men to pass the torch to. Anderson was one of these torches. He went on to do for other young men what Fuller did for him. By the close of his ministry, Anderson sent out sixteen men for the work of ministry[68] and regularly tried to correspond with them through letters.[69]

Conclusion

Fuller did not treat Anderson like a personal project. Their conversations and topics, for the most part, were everyday life. He rarely gave advice, but when he did, it was desired and listened to. He did not talk like Anderson was the young man in the relationship, and Fuller was the mentor. He spoke with him as a grown father talks to his son; he talked to him as a friend and co-laborer in the faith. He treated him with respect, as he indeed did highly respect Anderson.

In these letters, we see Fuller not primarily as the "elephant of Kettering"[70] or "the greatest theologian who ever served our denomination,"[71] but we see a Christian, and we see a friendship between two Christians. A good mentor,

---

[68] Anderson, *Life and Letters*, 375.

[69] See his letters to Thomas Swam and William Turnbull in Anderson, *Life and Letters*, 375–383.

[70] David Phillips, *Memoir of the Life, Labors, and Extensive Usefulness of the Rev. Christmas Evans* (New York: M.W. Dodd, 1843), 74.

[71] Cited in Gilbert Laws, *Andrew Fuller: Pastor, Theologian, Rope- holder* (London: Carey, 1942), 127.

Who Was Christopher Anderson?

Fuller shows, is not one always looking to instill wisdom at every moment, but is one who lives life with you, knows you, cares for you, and respects you.

Christopher Anderson is unknown to most Christians in the church; even among historians he is barely mentioned. Yet the words of Fuller about him ought to be heeded:

> He is a fine writer, a close thinker, a good preacher; and what is more, a holy, diligent, mild character. Indeed, should anything turn out for his leaving Edinburgh, I know he would be caught at by the first Churches of our denomination. ... If I dare try to remove him from Edinburgh, and could induce him to come and be co-pastor with me, I would divide my income with him; and he would take my place in the Mission, if he survived me; and he is not twenty-five years old.[72]

When a man of Andrew Fuller's stature had such high regard for a man that he desires him to replace him as pastor at Kettering and as secretary of the BMS, we would do well to pay attention and study the life and ministry of such a man.

---

[72] Fuller to Ward, December 10, 1807 in *Life and* Letters, 182-183.

1
Mr. Anderson to Mr. Fuller[1]

[1806?]

You mentioned some time ago that you were writing on the subject of preaching, or preaching Christ.[2] ... You know we have had a great deal of preaching in Scotland of late, and what may be called preaching Christ too, at least many seem to think no one preaches Christ so fully, freely, and simply, as they do themselves; yet, alas! since this sort of preaching has become the acmé with many, usefulness has appeared on the decline. To speak in Bunyan's[3] style, among our modern friends there seems to be nothing but illuminations and rejoicings, while they think all slings, and stones, and artillery unnecessary. I dare say you know what I mean. ... Our Antinomians (shall I call them? for I do not like to do so) in Scotland,[4] are argumentative, and hardy critics; and although they

---

[1] Anderson, *Life and Letters*, 68.

[2] See "Thoughts on Preaching" in *The Complete Works of the Rev. Andrew Fuller*, ed. Joseph Belcher (reprint; Harrisonburg: VA: Sprinkle, 1988), 1:712-727; "LXIX: Preaching Christ," *Complete Works*, 1:501-504. For a recent edition of both of these works in one volume see also Andrew Fuller, *Preaching* (Peterborough, ON: H&E Publishing, 2018). See also David E. Prince, *Preaching the truth as it is in Jesus: A reader on Andrew Fuller* (Peterborough, ON: H&E Publishing, 2022).

[3] John Bunyan (1628-1688). Oxford University Press has published a multi-volume critical edition of Bunyan's works. Banner of Truth have reprinted George Offor, *The Works of John Bunyan* (3 vols; Edinburgh: Banner of Truth, 1991 [orig.ed.1854]). There are many studies of Bunyan: Christopher Hill, *A Turbulent, Seditious and Factious People: John Bunyan and His Church* (Oxford: OUP, 1988) focusses on his place in radical Nonconformity. Richard Greaves, *Glimpses of Glory: John Bunyan and English Dissent* (Stanford: Stanford UP, 2002) has a larger focus on his personality and character. A biography of Bunyan that focusses on his preaching and writing style is Henri Talon, *John Bunyan: The Man and His Work* (London: Salisbury Square, 1951 [French ed. 1948]).

[4] It is probable that this reference is to the Scotch Baptists in Scotland, in particular their leader Archibald McLean. John Ryland, D.D., *Life and Death of the Rev*

do not deny the law of God, as some in England do, yet they seem to have a miserable want of faith in it to convict, or do any good in the way of conversion. In short, it is the simple truth, and this, it is to be feared, in their management, is nothing save a meagre, naked, isolated proposition. I believe your preachers also might improve, in holding forth the Saviour as the broad and exclusive ground of acceptance to the guilty, as the only way to be healed of their malady.

Andrew Fuller (London: Button & Son, 1818), 168, 170, 180-186. The views in question were earlier promulgated by John Glas (1695-1773) and his more famous son-in-law Robert Sandeman (1718-1771) who led a restorationist secession movement from the Church of Scotland that established places of worship throughout the United Kingdom and in a few other locations in North America. Its basic theology is Calvinistic, but it holds an intellectualist view of faith, stressing a simple act of belief in the resurrection of Jesus for salvation. Andrew Fuller wrote his *Strictures on Sandemanianism in Twelve Letters to a Friend* in 1810, in response to the views of Archibald McLean (1738-1812), the leading exponent of these views in Scottish Baptists ranks. For a modern critical edition of this work, see Nathan A. Finn (ed.), *The Complete Works of Andrew Fuller, Volume 9 Apologetic Works 5: Strictures on Sandemanianism* (Berlin /Boston: De Gruyter, 2016).

2
Mr. Anderson to Fuller[1]

August 18, 1807
Edinburgh

... I find my situation in some respects peculiar and difficult. May I not explain myself? I have no person as yet whom I can call a right-hand man, nor have I had one all along who could enter into my difficulties. But I can unbosom myself to you, and your advice, I know, will not be withheld.

When I gave up my worldly employment, and was afterwards led to cease from thinking of going to a warm climate,[2] my next immediate desire was to be useful at home. Having some little money of my own, I resolved to look about and not be too hasty in fixing on a situation which might be for life. Edinburgh presented itself, and seemed to claim my attention; you know under what circumstances. I have therefore tried, and, on the whole, had no occasion to repent, but to bless God for his kindness. My idea was to spend a part of what I had in supporting myself until it might please the Lord to raise up friends to whom this would be reckoned no burden. Someone seemed called on in this cause to make a small

---

[1] Anderson, *Life and Letters*, 75-77.

[2] Anderson had been committed to supporting the Particular Baptist Missionary Society since 1799, following Andrew Fuller's first visit to Edinburgh on behalf of that body. The death of his father had left him free to consider offering for service with the society in India. However, on health grounds he concluded that he was best able to support this cause while based in Edinburgh. See Hugh Anderson, *Life and Letters*, 25. Also Derek B. Murray, "Christopher Anderson and Scotland," in Donald E. Meek (ed.), *A Mind For Mission: Essays in appreciation of The Rev. Christopher Anderson (1782-1852)* (Edinburgh: The Scottish Baptist History Project, 1992), 4.

sacrifice, and to look to God for the issue. Perhaps this was I. I am still able to proceed in the same way, but shall not be always. And my difficulty is, what explanations would it be prudent to make?

Usefulness, I hope, however limited, is my great object. I am not then, my dear brother, writing anything under a wish to remove from an arduous, and in some respects a disheartening cause, but simply to know my way. The few who are with me are willing, I am persuaded, without having spoken of it, that I should become ultimately their pastor, and it may be that some advancement in this way is necessary to meet the increasing good pleasure of Jehovah; but then, I am bringing myself under closer engagements, the inability of others to support me in the cause may still continue, and spending more means in one experiment might appear, at some time hence, imprudent.

In general, most people seem to suppose when a person does anything for Jesus, he is only throwing the crumbs on the water and not his bread. It is not so with me at present, and I at times cannot prevent anxiety as to the issue on their account.

My friends, with one or two exceptions, are as yet ignorant of any difficulty in this respect, and, however willing, are inadequate to remove it. The love which they have for me seems sincere. Are not, then, the only two methods which I can adopt, to go on preaching as hitherto, without forming a closer connexion, until we have a more permanent prospect? or, to proceed in observing the Lord's Supper, in the faith of God appearing on our behalf? Which of these does my dear brother think most eligible? In either case, a few, perhaps all, must know the prospect before them—the possible alterna-

1807

tive. ... You know, I cannot have forgot England. I love you and many of the friends in your country. My heart was refreshed, while I have every reason to think my labour was not in vain to others. Yet all this would only make me look forward to the pleasure of sitting down with you before the throne; but I saw places poor and needy, and sheep looking up in various quarters, and not fed, it may be, for want of supply. I have remembered the happiness of having from 300 to 700 hearers, and really have been unable to free myself occasionally from a little depression of spirits in going from Sabbath to Sabbath to preach to 70, 100, or 200, several of these having come from curiosity, and others to criticise. This, along with a divisive spirit, which, alas! seems too much to pervade this place now, sometimes perplexes me for hours, and takes sleep from my eyes. Yet again, I am afraid, I am not thankful enough to God, and too blind to perceive the advantages of my situation, with the need of patience. I am willing to labour for years, had I no reason to doubt of my being in the path of duty. I am not constitutionally given to look on the dark side, and not very apt to faint at a few discouragements. I beg you will excuse this long letter. Half-an-hour under your mulberry tree would have rendered it unnecessary, but that is now impracticable. I should be glad of a letter from you—indeed, I shall feel somewhat anxious till I hear from you. Do not suppose from the general tenor of this that I am discouraged—no—by no means. ... May the love of the Spirit at all seasons be with you!

3
Mr. Fuller to Anderson[1]

September 1, 1807
Kettering

My very dear brother,

I must sit down and talk with you an hour, though not under the mulberry tree. The things which exercise your mind are those which have exercised mine on your behalf. When we gave you up for India,[2] it was from pure love to Edinburgh. ... Were I now disposed to try and draw you from the north, I could mention stations of promising usefulness, but I will only say, if after trying your utmost, you should be obliged to give up, do not do so without first informing me. I am really at a loss as to advising you on the question—shall I form a church and be their pastor, or, shall I stay longer as I am? The former would be more likely to promote increase. On the other hand, who can advise his dear brother to cast his bread on the waters? If he does so, it must be his own choice. When I first began preaching it was at Soham.[3] There was a little church, and my heart was united to them. I became their pastor in 1775. In 1776 I married. My family increased, and I began to sink my little property. In another year or two, I should have sunk it

---

[1] Anderson, *Life and Letters*, 77-78.

[2] After Fuller's first visit on behalf of the Particular Baptist Missionary Society to Edinburgh in 1799, Christopher Anderson seriously considered offering to serve with the mission in India. See Murray, "Christopher Anderson and Scotland" in Meek (ed.), *A Mind For Mission*, 4.

[3] J.W. Morris, *Memoirs of the Life and Writings of the Rev. Andrew Fuller* (London, 1816), 20-24; Ryland, *Andrew Fuller*, 41-43.

all, and perhaps been unable to pay my way. I had only 200 people, or thereabouts. My religious acquaintance in the country thought I ought to remove. I was invited to Kettering, to London, and to some other places. I chose the first as being the least lucrative, and as affording a good prospect of usefulness. In 1782 I came hither,[4] but after having been connected with the church at Soham seven years, it caused a wound in my heart which seven more years did not heal. Yet, in reviewing it, I question if much of my pain did not arise from a youthful attachment to place and persons, which, however wisely planted in our minds, is not religion. Honour God, my dear brother, and he will honour you.

... I do not know enough of your circumstances to be able to speak of the propriety of your continuing to sink property. If what you have be considerable, a part might be spared. But if this be not the case, though you should settle as a pastor, there may come a time, and that at no great distance, when you may be obliged to remove. Yet, should this be the case, the consciousness of having done your utmost, will be a satisfaction; and stations in England will not be wanting where they would gladly support you for your services in the ministry. Grace and peace be with you.

A. Fuller

---

[4] Morris, *Andrew Fuller*, 35-39; Ryland, *Andrew Fuller*, 43-70.

4
Mr. Anderson to Mr. Fuller[1]

November 1807

Our little cause does not decline; attendance, indeed, is irregular, but usefulness is not at an end—and faith, patience, and prudence, did I possess them, may be able to effect more at a future day than was at first expected by some. ... I have baptized none but such as have lately been brought out of darkness, nor have I been applied to by any others. I should wish that we got the character of being most anxious about such—that we appeared to be a terror to Satan's power chiefly, and not the objects of jealousy, but of affectionate regard to surrounding Christians.

---

[1] Anderson, *Life and Letters*, 78-79.

5
Mr. Fuller to Mr. Anderson[1]

February 16, 1808
Kettering

My dear brother,

And so you are become a pastor of this little Church![2] Well, God be with you! I will now tell you what has been in my heart, but which I dared not mention while your mind was undecided. I have desired, and my friends have desired a plurality of pastors at Kettering, not for the sake of plurality, but because there is more work than I can do. And I have often wished to divide my income with you. It has seemed to me, that in you I should have a successor in the work of the Mission, should you survive me, as well as a faithful and affectionate brother in the Church. But now, it seems, my hopes are at an end. Well, all is right that God doth. May the work of the Lord prosper in your hand.

Having been for the last six weeks employed in answering just that number of pamphlets against the Mission, full of the venom of the old serpent, and having not yet finished my labour, I can only add a few lines.[3]

I do not know what to say as yet about a journey to Scotland. I feel a revolting at coming at all. I seem as if my old

---

[1] Anderson, *Life and Letters*, 183–184.
[2] Anderson was officially called by the church at Richmond Court to be their pastor and ordained on January 21, 1808. See Anderson, *Life and Letters*, 79, 82.
[3] See Belcher, *Complete Works of the Rev. Andrew Fuller*, 2:763–806.

friends at Edinburgh will be cool.[4] I do not know whether I shall not give it up. I am not able to travel and labour as I have done. But I shall see Brother Sutcliff,[5] and talk about it.

I have written thirty-two pages of remarks upon Mr. Ewing's[6] book, and six or seven more of the kind, and sent them a week ago to Dr. S.[7] Amongst them are seven or eight pages, containing my reasons for considering the time for celebrating the Lord's Supper as undetermined, only that it be *often*. I think we eat it often, but you oftener; we do well, but perhaps you do better; but neither of us act contrary to the institution of Christ. Mr. M'L.[8] and Mr. J. Haldane[9] deny that 1 Cor. 11:26 proves that it ought to be often, and that if not weekly, it might as well be only once a year, or in seven years. But I have endeavoured to prove that the comparative always

---

[4] This is a reference to Fuller's theological disagreements with some of the views of Scotch Baptist Minister Archibald McLean.

[5] John Sutcliff (1752-1814). He was the minister of Olney Baptist Church in Buckinghamshire. See Michael A.G. Haykin, *One Heart and One Soul: John Sutcliff of Olney, His friends and His times* (Darlington: Evangelical Press, 1995).

[6] Greville Ewing (1767-1841). He was a leading Congregational Minister in Scotland. He had been a colleague of Robert and James Alexander Haldane in their evangelistic ministry and church-planting efforts up to 1808. They parted company when the Haldanes adopted Baptist convictions in 1808. The standard biography of his life is J.J. Matheson, *Memoir of Greville Ewing* (London: John Snow, 1843).

[7] Charles Stuart of Edinburgh (1745-1826). He was a former Church of Scotland Minister, but adopted Baptist convictions in 1776. He worked closely with Andrew Fuller in support of BMS and was a prominent Evangelical figure active in Scotland. See N.R. Needham, "Stuart, Charles, of Dunearn (1745-1826)," in N.M. de S. Cameron (et al eds), *Dictionary of Scottish Church History and Theology* (*DSCHT*) (Edinburgh: T & T Clark, 1993), 803. Two of Andrew Fuller's letters to Stuart are found in Michael A.G. Haykin, *The Armies of the Lamb: The Spirituality of Andrew Fuller* (Dundas, ON: Joshua Press, 2001), 59-74.

[8] Archibald McLean (1733-1812). For fuller details on his life see William Jones, *Works of Archibald McLean* (London: William Jones, 1823), "Memoir of the Author," 6:ix-cxxxii. The most recent biographical study is Brian Talbot, "Archibald McLean (1733-1812)" in Michael A.G. Haykin, *The British Particular Baptists* (Springfield, MO: Particular Baptist Press, 2019), 5:64-89.

[9] James Haldane (1768-1851). The standard biography is Alexander Haldane, *The Lives of Robert and James Haldane* (Edinburgh: Banner of Truth, 1990 [Orig.ed. 1852]).

suppose the positive; or that the phrase, *as often as*, which goes to determine the frequency of a thing by some other thing, supposes both to be frequent. The comparative mode of speaking relates to the degree of frequency; but it were absurd to talk of degrees of frequency where no frequency is. It would not be said, as oft, if it were not *oft*. My Christian love to Brother Barclay.[10] Affectionately yours,

A. Fuller

P.S. Mr. Hall[11] is much pleased at the idea of you and Barclay going to Ireland.[12] He is married, and settles at Leicester. There is a great gathering under his preaching. He is more and more evangelical and spiritual.

---

[10] George Barclay (1774-1838) was the Minister of Irvine Baptist Church and the most influential "English" Baptist Minister in Scotland at the beginning of the nineteenth century. He mentored Christopher Anderson in his earlier years and subsequently worked closely with him in home and overseas mission endeavours. See Brian Talbot, "George Barclay (1994-1838)" in Haykin, *British Particular Baptists*, 5:400-424. For more information on the "English" Baptists in Scotland, see Brian R. Talbot, *Search for a Common Identity: The Origins of the Baptist Union of Scotland, 1800-1870* (Carlisle, PA: Paternoster Press, 2003), 115-152.

[11] Robert Hall Jr (1764-1831) married in 1808. He was Minister of Harvey Lane Baptist Church, Leicester from 1807-1826. "A Brief Memoir of The Rev. Robert Hall, A.M." is contained in O. Gregory (ed.), *The Works of Robert Hall A.M.* (6 Vols; London: Holdsworth and Ball, 1833), 6:1-141.

[12] Information from Anderson's 1814 tour of Ireland and the ongoing interest he showed in Ireland is given in Anderson, *Life and Letters*, 123-124, 134-156. George Barclay and Christopher Anderson had both been concerned for some years about the spiritual welfare of Ireland, alongside English Baptist colleagues such as John Saffery of Salisbury. A report of Saffery and Barclay's July 1813 tour of Ireland, for example, is given in J. Saffery, "State of Religion in Ireland," Sep. 6, 1813, *The Baptist Magazine for 1813* (Vol V, October 1813), 432-434. The significance of Saffery's letter in leading to the formation of the Baptist Irish Society in April 1814 is given in, J. Belcher D.D. & A.G. Fuller, *The Baptist Irish Society* (London: Houston and Stoneman, 1845), 2-5.

6
Mr. Anderson to Mr. Fuller[1]

July 1, 1808
Edinburgh

My dear brother,

I am sorry indeed that the effects of this accident still continue to linger about you. I shall live in the hope of seeing you, however, about September if the Lord will. Well, I think Barclay[2] and I should go. We propose to leave this so as to be in Ireland the first Lord's Day in August. I was pleased with the manner in which my few friends spoke of the proposal. At first they seemed surprised, and a few revolted at the very idea; but finally, after time to think and pray over it, they not only acquiesced, but wished me to go. I am glad to hear your account on Mr. Hall. This happy improvement commenced immediately after his recovery from his last illness. I have not forgotten, nor, it may be, shall ever forget his humble solemn manner of his praying then. He made me feel towards God in a way I had been formerly almost ignorant of—reverential fear, or the homage of prostration. I shall be happy to see his reply to the black inspiration of the *Edinburgh Review*. I and my country are guiltless. We are indebted to an Englishman[3]

---

[1] Anderson, *Life and Letters*, 185.

[2] Barclay and Anderson had been particularly active in the early nineteenth century in support of Baptist work in Ireland. On this mission agency see also John H.Y. Briggs, *English Baptists of the 19th Century* (Didcot: Baptist Historical Society, 1994), 299; and especially Belcher and Fuller, *Baptist Irish Society: Its Origins, History and Prospects*.

[3] Sydney Smith, a High Church Episcopalian, wrote disapprovingly of both Baptists in general and of their Indian Mission. Sydney Smith, "Indian Missions," *Edin-*

(alas! that it should be so) for those expectorations. May the Lord sanctify all his dealings with you, my ever dear brother. But (as Cowper[4] said to one of his friends) you must not die yet, for we can by no means do without you.

Yours, &c.,

Christ[topher] Anderson

---

burgh *Review* 12 (April 1808): 158, 162. See Brian R. Talbot, *Building on a Common Foundation: The Baptist Union of Scotland 1869-2019* (Eugene, OR: Pickwick Publications, 2021), 1-5 for the wider context of this publication.

[4] William Cowper (1731-1800) was a well-known poet and hymn writer. For a detailed biography of Cowper, see George M. Ella, *William Cowper: Poet of Paradise* (Darlington: Evangelical Press, 1993).

7
Mr. Fuller to Mr. Anderson[1]

February 21, 1809
Kettering

I have had much to do on the Mission business respecting the Bible Society. It was a painful burden to be obliged to go and state the truth. But I think they have acted honourably, whatever be the issue.

I bless God for your increase. I also have a little boy, a nephew, whom I expect shortly to baptise with perhaps some others. Joseph Fuller,[2] that is his name, has nearly mastered the Latin and Greek in the last year. I hope his is born for some good.

The *Baptist Magazine* sells 4000 they say, yet it disgusts most thinking people. I know of no "talents" among them, except Steadman.[3] There is a want of modesty, and too much made of baptism.

---

[1] Anderson, *Life and Letters*, 187-188.

[2] Joseph Fuller (c.1794-d.1812) was baptised by Fuller on April 30, 1809 at Kettering, at the age of fifteen. He would die three years later on March 23, 1812 in Little Bentley, Essex. See "A Memoir of Mr. Joseph Fuller," *The Baptist Magazine* 5 (February 1813): 45-49. See also John Ryland, *The Work of Faith: the Labour of Love, and the Patience of Hope, Illustrated in the Life and Death of Rev. Andrew Fuller* (Charlestown: Samuel Etheridge, 1818), 293-299.

[3] William Steadman (1764-1837), was the pastor of Westgate Baptist Church, in Bradford, Yorkshire, and President of the Northern Baptist Education Society. See Sharon James, "William Steadman (1764-1837)," in Haykin (ed.), *British Particular Baptists*, 2:162-181.

Poor Dublin! I do not understand what P.[4] means by "a few of them changing the order of the church government," unless it be to admit of open communion; and this will not save Swift's Alley. If any good is done, it must be by someone raised up on purpose.[5]

Affectionately yours,

A. Fuller

---

[4] It is quite likely that "P" is Samuel Pearce. He had shown a keen interest in Irish Baptists and their witness and had visited this church in Dublin. See "Samuel Pearce and the stirring of English interest" in Crawford Gribben, *The Revival of Particular Baptist Life in Ireland 1780-1840* (Dunstable: Fauconberg Press, 2011), 8-15.

[5] The Swift's Alley Baptist Church in Dublin had been erected in 1653 under the leadership of Thomas Patient. The congregation struggled to continue its witness in the nineteenth century. The building was sold to the Episcopal Church in 1835. Kevin Herlihy, *The Irish Dissenting Tradition 1650-1750* (Dublin: Four Courts Press, 1995), 53-55. For the broader difficulties for Irish Baptists in establishing their witness in Ireland, see pages 65-80.

8
Mr. Fuller to Mr. Anderson[1]

May 1809

... There is a dreadful crash at Dunstable. M[orris] has failed, and his ministry is at an end![2]

---

[1] Anderson, *Life and Letters*, 188.

[2] "M" is John Webster Morris (1763-1836). See Michael A.G. Haykin, *One Heart and One Soul: John Sutcliff of Olney, his friends and his times* (Darlington: Evangelical Press, 1994), 279-286 for a full account of Morris' ministry and later reluctant departure from it in 1809. However, it was Morris' unwillingness to admit his faults in the years that followed that led to a breach in the friendship with Fuller and other former colleagues. An attempted reconciliation was made by Fuller in December 1811, but it was unsuccessful. Morris was originally a journeyman printer from Norfolk, who was called to the pastorate of Clipstone Baptist Church in Northamptonshire in 1785. He pastored that church until 1803. Morris was also very active in working with other colleagues such as Andrew Fuller and William Carey in the early years of the BMS. He then moved to Bedfordshire where he served from 1803 to 1809 in the joint charge over Baptist causes in Thorn, Houghton, and Dunstable. Charles E. Duffey, *Houghton Regis Baptist Church Diamond Jubilee of the Present Chapel* (1925), 4-5. See also William Perkins, "Morris, John Webster (1763-1836)," *Dictionary of National Biography*, 13:998. An account of Morris' life, and especially a comparative study of his biography of Andrew Fuller with that written by John Ryland, is given in Ryan Griffith's, "'Promoting Pure and Undefiled Religion': John Ryland, JR. (1753-1825) and Edwardsean Biography" (PhD thesis, The Southern Baptist Theological Seminary, Louisville, Kentucky, 2017), 212-248. A recently published critical edition of the Fuller biography by Ryland, together with comparative comments on Morris' biography of him is: C. Ryan Griffiths, *The Life of Andrew Fuller: A Critical Edition of John Ryland's Biography* (Berlin/Boston: De Gruyters, 2021).

9
Mr. Anderson to Mr. Fuller[1]

June 30, 1809
Edinburgh

My friend Burnett[2] and I got safe home on Friday after we parted from you. He has returned to his estate in Aberdeenshire, but I expect to see him again in Edinburgh before long, ... I have received the *Periodical Accounts*.[3] Oh, what men are these! Their humility and wisdom, zeal and love, how uncommon! One of them complains of the cold language of England. And cannot England then take fire, complain for herself, and cry that her language is too poor to express her experience of the love of Christ? Alas, no! Charm they ever so wisely, she says the men are "mad."

The sober proportions of her sons look into the sacred volume, and find it to abound with strong Eastern metaphor—that the love of Christ is not a lofty subject—that the language of the East has gone beyond all the bounds of propriety and reason. We must neither go as far as Revelation would lead us, nor conceive the subject so vast as it insinuates or asserts.

---

[1] Anderson, *Life and Letters*, 189-190.

[2] John Burnett of Kemnay, who was converted under Anderson' ministry and then became a member of Anderson's church in Edinburgh, owned an estate in Kemnay, Aberdeenshire. Burnett delighted in accompanying Anderson in evangelistic preaching tours. See Derek B. Murray, "The Burnetts of Kemnay—two Nineteenth Century Baptist Lairds," unpublished 2013 paper. For more details on this family see Susan Burnett (of Kemnay), *Without Fanfare, the story of my family* (Kemnay: Kemnay House Publications, 1994).

[3] These are the BMS reports of work in India.

I hope you will get another Number published soon, though it were but a sixpenny one. Though you were not to give so much news, the kind of matter you have in store seems admirably calculated to enhance the Mission in the esteem of the godly. I hope you will certainly publish the *case of restoration to the church*,[4] that of poor Deep Chundra, and Brother Carey's address to him when re-admitted. It is not only very affecting and calculated to do good to backsliders in general, but it will show the *Scotch* what sort of discipline we have among us.[5]

---

[4] Deep Chundra was baptised by Carey on profession of faith on January 6, 1805. See *Periodic Accounts Relative to the Baptist Missionary Society* (London: Burditt and Morris,1810), 4:x. It was reported he had "gone back into idolatry" (513), but details of his restoration to the Christian faith were given in a letter of from Joshua Rowe in Serampore to a Mrs S. of Bristol, dated Nov.29, 1808. *Periodical Accounts, No XIX,* from April to December 1808, 549–551. [The page numbers are from bound volume III of *Periodic Accounts* covering reports from June 1804 to December 1808.

[5] The Scotch Baptists had strict church discipline and struggled to forbear with one another over differences in beliefs or practices. See Talbot, *Search for a Common Identity*, 57-70.

10
Mr. Anderson to Mr. Fuller[1]
[on the death of his niece]

August 18, 1809
Edinburgh

My beloved brother Fuller,

The Lord has been pleased, in his all-wise Providence, to bring my sister-in-law and myself into peculiar trial. A most beloved child, whom you took up in your arms and kissed when in my house, has been called to glory in about ten days illness. We had no idea that this would prove mortal so soon. She was, it may be said, but a niece, yes, but such a niece! Her father one of the most active and amiable of saints, died about seven years ago. So ardent was the affection of his wife, that though cheerful and submissive as a Christian, to this day she is wont to weep at the remembrance of him. And now this dear child, in whose life her own was bound up, and to whom your brother acted in the capacity of a father, is departed. ... We are perverse creatures, and apt, alas! to convert that into matter of regret which is ground for praise. She was nine years of age, a most interesting period of life for a child to die; but she was a Christian for many a day, I believe, before she died. Laying the partiality of friendship aside, which no doubt must be difficult, I am inclined to think the evidence such as is scarcely to be found in infant years. Being in the days of health, when all was well, it is of the most unsuspicious kind,

---

[1] Anderson, *Life and Letters*, 158–160.

and affords far more consolation than expressions uttered in the prospect of death. I may one day trouble you with some anecdotes. She was given to prayer morning and evening, for about three years past, and took such delight in reading her Bible, that I was often pleased and affected by it. One morning I was so struck that, "O child!" thought I, "you seem to love your Bible more than your uncle does, who is a preacher of the Gospel."

I shall only mention the following little tale, as an evidence of her mind being imbued with divine knowledge. She was fond of reading the Old Testament; and talking with her mother one day when doing so about the children of Israel's conduct in the wilderness, their unbelief and rebellion, she expressed her wonder at the Lord's patience, and added, "there were only two of them allowed to enter the land of Canaan." "Yes," said her mother, "I dare say, Jeannie, you think these Israelites were very wicked people, and that we are not so bad as they were." "O no, mother!" she replied, "I do not think that, but it shows how true that is, "Strait is the gate and narrow is the way that leadeth unto life, and few there be that find it."[2] Perhaps were her sayings remembered, they would present a wonderful picture of a child, but her conduct is that which will endear her memory to me to the end of my days. It may appear strange that I should be so overcome. ... but I am writing to a beloved brother, who, I know well, has drunk deep in the cup of trial. You will overlook my weakness ... O that it may be sanctified to my dear sister! It is truly affecting to see her at one time distracted with her loss, then distressed at her own state of mind as not more submissive, then recounting the evidence of the child's

---

[2] Matthew 7:14.

1809

faith, hope, and love, and becoming more composed. The numerous days to which her grief may extend renders her a tender charge. And now, dear brother, could you spare a little time to write a letter of consolation to a widow bereaved of her only child? I admire her Christianity, indeed, very much. Remember me at a throne of grace.

11
Mr. Fuller to Mr. Anderson[1]

August 22, 1809
Kettering

My dear brother,

I doubt not but this beloved child had a deep interest in your heart, and the bereavement to your dear sister must be very severe. Make my sympathizing regards to her. If you were not Christians, or the child had given no hope of her Christianity, the case had been extremely different.

I seldom hear of such bereavements, without thinking of Aaron's words to Moses in Leviticus 10:19: "Such things have befallen me!" I have lost an affectionate wife and fourteen children.[2] The heaviest loss among the children was a little girl between six and seven, of whose Christianity, nevertheless, I had considerable hopes.[3]

In looking minutely into the things that befell Aaron, I have found matter of consolation. He lost two sons in one day, and under circumstances much more distressing than

---

[1] Anderson, *Life and Letters*, 160-162.

[2] The details are given in Ryland, *Life and Death of the Rev, Andrew Fuller* (1818), 268 (the death of first wife Sarah Gardiner and nine of her children); 295 (the death in infancy of three children born to his second wife Ann Coles, and the later death of the elder daughter from this marriage); 300, the death of a son who had caused much grief to Fuller by some of his actions.

There is some discrepancy between the different accounts of how many children Fuller lost. The Family Tree would number 10 lost in infancy, and Ryland recorded 11. But here, Fuller says 14. It may be that Fuller had a slip of the pen, or it could be that the 14 Fuller mentions here is a more personal narrative, including those who were not born—miscarriages.

[3] Sarah Fuller; the details are given in Ryland, *Life and Death of the Rev, Andrew Fuller* (1818), 270-285.

anything I ever met with. The very day before their death, both he and the young men seemed to be in all their glory. They presented the offerings of the people to the Lord; Aaron lifted up his hand toward the people and blessed them; and both Moses and Aaron went into the tabernacle, and the glory of the Lord appeared unto all; their offering was accepted, and they shouted and fell on their faces.[4] Next to Moses and Aaron, none stood higher, or were more likely to be honourable, than Nadab and Abihu. Yet, lo! the next day they are slain, and that not in an ordinary way, but with signal marks of the divine displeasure, and with every appearance of dying in their sins! Such things, my dear friends! have not befallen me or you. Yet "Aaron held his peace"![5]

I have also found the Lamentations of Jeremiah, especially chapter 3:1-36, very profitable in times of affliction. Conceive of that plaintive book as written for the use of the captives in Babylon. In the first twenty-one verses the Prophet seems to review his own troubles during the course of his prophesying, and to hold up the use they had been to him for their example. Let me request you and your dear sister to read this chapter with me for half an hour. You will see in verses 1-18, what had been his sore complaints. But in verses 19-21, we find that he had since reviewed them, and derived good from them. He had learned a lesson of humility and of hope. The very remembrance of his afflictions affected and humbled him, for they had, no doubt, afforded large proof of his weakness and sinfulness, and by leading him to inquire wherefore the Lord had thus contended with him, furnished many evidences of the corruption of his nature. And while they humbled him,

---

[4] Leviticus 9:15-24.
[5] Leviticus 10:3.

1809

they furnished him with fresh hope, for he would find that though he had considered his afflictions as intolerable, yet he had been enabled to bear them, and was thus far carried through them. From verses 22-36, he seems directly to address the captives; teaching them, that deplorable as their condition was, it might have been worse; that after losing their children in the war and in the siege (see 4:2-12), their liberty, their country, and all the privileges of Zion, yet they had not lost their God![6] that it was good to hope, and quietly wait for his salvation; yea, that it was good to bear the yoke, and that not only when growing old, to meeten them for another world. Sanctified afflictions seclude from injurious company, humble our aspiring spirits, and render us meek and patient. Finally, he teaches them that God would not afflict forever, and while he did so, it was not without a cause.

If these sentiments were drunk in by the captives, though they might not produce joy, yet they would soften and sweeten grief; and I doubt not they would have the same effect on my dear friends under their bereavement.

That man is said to be blessed who brings forth fruit in his season.[7] Perhaps you never had such an opportunity before of showing the reality of your faith, and the efficacy of your hope. Temptations and severe afflictions are the seasons in which God looks for fruit. If we are not rendered more humble, more patient, and more spiritually-minded under them, it is not likely that we shall be so under the smiles of prosperity.

Grace and peace be with you and your affectionate brother.

A. Fuller

---

[6] Jeremiah 4:24.
[7] Psalm 1:3.

12
Mr. Anderson to Mr. Fuller[1]

April 22, 1810
Edinburgh

My dear brother,
I regret much that I have been detained so long from writing you. While engaged in printing the *Brief Narrative*,[2] it occurred to me that a map was much wanting to the *Periodical Accounts*. The expense, though considerable, seemed no object, and in this case the projection would, of course, be gratis. I have therefore drawn two; they are attached to the octavo edition, which, when done up neatly, will sell for two shillings. This is considered reasonable, if not cheap. The first is a map of Bengal on a large scale, with the roads and inland navigation; the other is a map of the languages of the East, pointing out by dotted lines and colouring, the seat and reputed boundary of the various language. The list of the baptized at the end of the *Narrative*, I have made more particular, through the assistance of Mr. Ward's[3] book and the *Periodical Accounts*. I sent a few of the octavo Narrative last week among some of the Directors of our Bible Society, and at our monthly

---

[1] Anderson, *Life and Letters*, 190–191.
[2] Christopher Anderson, *Brief Narrative of the Baptist Mission in India* (1808; 3rd edition, 1810).
[3] William Ward's journal is one of the most important sources of information on BMS work in India. William Carey's colleague wrote the first entry on May, 25, 1799, and the last on October 30, 1811. See E. Daniel Potts, "William Ward's Missionary Journal," *Baptist Quarterly* 25.3 (1973): 111–114. It was a key source for John Clark Marshman's *The Life and Times of Carey, Marshman And Ward*, 2 Vols. (London: Longman, Brown, Green, Longman & Roberts, 1859).

meeting on Monday I had the pleasure of receiving a vote of £200 to the Translations. I have received some other sums, an account of which, together with a list of the names as they should be printed in the next Number, I shall send in a few days, if the Lord will. After paying for the *Narrative*, I shall have a considerable balance to remit. ... If you approve, I propose that the next Number of the *Periodical Accounts*, beginning the fourth volume, be accompanied with the same maps. The plates will bear 3000 to 4000 impressions, and the whole accounts will be rendered more intelligible to many. If you determine on this, after seeing the *Narrative*, the impressions will be best thrown off and coloured here and sent to London.

I thank you, my dear friend, for your "Letters." They are to me sweet; to others they will be otherwise. What is one man's food is another's poison. "I hope" said I to Dr. S.[4] on the street the other day, "they will do much good." "They will do much mischief," said he, "in the first place." I could plainly perceive that he, good man, felt at somewhat. It may be you have fallen foul of some favourite tenet which has grown with his growth, and strengthened with his strength.

---

[4] Charles Stuart.

13
Mr. Fuller to Mr. Anderson[1]

May 17, 1810
Kettering

… I have just received the parcel of *Brief Narrative*,[2] and like the maps much—wish you immediately to get 3000 of these maps struck off and sent up to go into the *Periodical Accounts*, No. XX. I have only to add a packet of love from Burls',[3] Burditt's,[4] &c, and from none more than from your affectionate brother,

A. Fuller

---

[1] Anderson, *Life and Letters*, 191-192.
[2] Christopher Anderson, *Brief Narrative of the Baptist Mission in India* (London, Button, 1808).
[3] William Burls was a BMS agent in London in Fuller's lifetime and later BMS Treasurer from 1819-1821.
[4] J. Burditt was the joint publisher of *The Baptist Magazine* with W. Button in their premises in Paternoster Row, London, from its launch in 1809.

14
Mr. Fuller to Mr. Anderson[1]

May 17, 1811
Kettering

Present my thanks to the Committee of the Bible Society for this second instance of their generosity. Will thank you to remit it to Mr. King[2] of Birmingham, as our funds are more than exhausted.

I *must* postpone my journey for a while. I have not preached since the 21st of April. It is very much like a cold I took in 1801, and goes off very slow. I ride out every forenoon, but the least fresh cold goes to my lungs. I have nearly lost my hearing.

The failure of animal spirits at my time of life, especially under this affliction, has led me to question whether a considerable part of my religious zeal, both in and out of the pulpit, has not consisted in them. I want to bring forth those *fruits* which a season of affliction and advance in life require.

Lord's-day Morning, 19 May.—A strong fever last night. Got no sleep till two or three this morning. Cannot so much as attend public worship today.

---

[1] Anderson, *Life and Letters*, 192-193.
[2] Almost certainly Thomas King, the treasurer of the Birmingham auxiliary society of BMS and a deacon of Canon Street Baptist Church in that city where Samuel Pearce served as the pastor. King was also BMS treasurer for some years prior to his death in 1831. For more details see W. Finnemore, *The Story of a Hundred Years, 1823-1923: Being the Centenary Booklet of the Birmingham Auxiliary of the Baptist Missionary Society* (Oxford: Oxford University Press, 1923), 21-22.

15
Mr. Fuller to Mr. Anderson[1]

December 4, 1811
Kettering

I duly received your draft of £42, 12s. 4d., and a bill of £262, 2s. 6d., and for all your labours of love do most cordially thank you.

Poor M[orris]! he is now on a visit at Rowell, and wants to see me. I have just now written my friend, at whose house he is, and who invited me to dine with him today, that if after reading *the inclosed note*, Mr. M. wished to see me, I would try and go over tomorrow.

—N.B. This enclosed note is in short hand, addressed to Mr. M[orris]. Its contents are these:

Copy of Supposed Letters[2]

My dear brother,

I have sinned against the Lord, and he has laid his hand upon me. I was lifted up, and he has cast me down. Instead of accepting the punishment of mine iniquity, I have been laying the blame on others. I have dishonoured God, and reduced my brethren to the situation of having no comfort in my concerns but by endeavouring

---

[1] Anderson, *Life and Letters*, 193–194.
[2] Anderson, *Life and Letters*, 194.

to forget them. I have been trying to justify myself, but I will do so no more.³

Answer

My dear brother,

I also am a sinner, deeply indebted to mercy. If the above be your sentiments, we will weep over one another, and the days of past friendship and affection shall be revived.

Yes, I think of printing on the Revelation some time, but not just yet. The copy is ready, only I wish to read and think a little more.⁴ I am much of opinion at present that we may be towards 200 years ere we arrive at the millennium; and that the present is *the period of the vials*. I believe it will be during *this period* that the Gospel will prevail over Paganism, Mahometanism, Apostate Judaism, Popery, &c. This will be a

---

³ Morris in his Memoir of Fuller, alongside many commendatory comments, makes this statement about how Fuller handled the shortcomings of others: "Instead of seeking that which is gone astray and binding up that which is broken; his dispensatory contained no emollients, and he seemed to have no idea that a wound could be healed, except by the immediate application of a caustic…" Morris, *Memoirs of Andrew Fuller*, 490–491.

⁴ It was as late as 1815, at the urging of the Baptist church in Kettering, before Fuller was finally persuaded to publish his *Expository Discourses on The Apocalypse*. See Belcher (ed), *Complete Works of the Rev Andrew Fuller*, 3:201-307. Andrew Fuller, in line with the vast majority of the new missionary movement supporters held to a post-millennial understanding of the end times. A representative study of this perspective from a contemporary colleague came from Independent Minister David Bogue, *Discourses on the Millennium* (London: T. Hamilton, 1818). A study of the broader support for this position is found in Iain Murray, *The Puritan Hope: Revival and the Interpretation of Prophecy* (Edinburgh: Banner of Truth, 1985).

See also Crawford Gribben, Andrew Fuller and the millennium, *Jonathan Edwards Online Journal* 10.2 (October 2020): 190-192. For a critical edition see Andrew Fuller, *The Complete Works of Andrew Fuller. Volume 15: Expository Discourses on the Apocalypse*, ed. Crawford Gribben (Berlin: DeGruter, 2022).

period for *conflict and victory*; the millennium for *real*—that is as the reign of David; this, of Solomon.

I was in London in the beginning of November, and caught cold in returning, which works much as my cold did last spring. I am obliged to be daily taking medicine, and sometimes can get no sleep till two or three in the morning.

I am affectionately yours,

A. Fuller

16
Mr. Anderson to Mr. Fuller[1]

December 10, 1811
Edinburgh

I have your notes on Revelations curiously last night. Man is an impatient creature. The husbandman waiteth for the precious fruits of the earth;[2] he is obliged to do so; were nature in his power we should see strange doings. I have heard of a man, the good John Newton,[3] that if you told him when you put the most to the fire, so that he could plant his salad at the same time, it was ready before the most was roasted. But this, he added, is not God's method. I have been led to these rambling remarks by your placing the millennium at the distance of 200 years. Some very good people of the present day would be much disposed to put to a petition and say, "Oh, try if you can bring it a little nearer." So anxious are we too frequently to see "sights" rather than attend to present duty. As for myself, I have not made prophecy so much my study as to have a fixed opinion. There is a deliberate dignity and composure about the procedure of Jehovah which renders extremely probable your millennium. We see enough, however, to make our hearts grow big with anticipation, swell with gratitude, and rejoice with exceeding great joy.

---

[1] Anderson, *Life and Letters*, 194–195.
[2] James 5:7.
[3] John Newton (1725-1807) was a well-known Anglican Clergyman who had served at Olney in Buckinghamshire (1764-1780) and then at St. Mary Woolnoth in London (1780-1807). He was the author of "Amazing Grace," and a good friend and correspondent of many Nonconformist ministers.

I wish poor Mr. M[orris] may "come to himself," but, alas! apostasy is an awful thing. Oh, how dreadful for a man so to act as that even though he relent and return to God, he can scarcely be consistent without walking the remainder of his days in the bitterness of his soul. Restoration to the Divine favour, as rich, as full as formerly may take place, but a return to the confidential love and unlimited approbation of the saved is, I suppose, rarely if ever witnessed. O let integrity and truth keep me!

17
Mr. Fuller to Mr. Anderson[1]

December 31, 1811
Kettering

Last night I received by the mail from Sunderland a book which I left there, given me by Dr. Stuart. It is "McLean on the Hebrews."[2] There seems to be some good work in it, though it is not very accurately printed. When you or Dr. Stuart send me anything, put the "Abstract of the Revelation," which I lent him, into the parcel, and direct it to me to be left at Lothbury.

Poor M! it seems as if he cannot be willing to be saved by grace. I offered him a full and free forgiveness if he would only subscribe the note I sent him; but that, it seems, implies a "sweeping censure!" Only acknowledge thine iniquity! Ah, there is the hinge—but how hard to a proud spirit! Our town was all in terror the other day by the horrible speeches of a dying sinner, who seemed in hell while yet on earth—driven away in his wickedness and without hope.

27th January 1812.—I have just returned from London, and must direct this to you at Liverpool. The London ministers want to get the *Baptist Magazine* to London. Ivimey[3] of

---

[1] Anderson, *Life and Letters*, 195-198.

[2] Archibald McLean, *A Paraphrase and Commentary on the Epistle to the Hebrews* (2 vols; Edinburgh, 1811-1817); 2nd edition revised (2 vols; London, 1820).

[3] Joseph Ivimey (1773-1834) was the pastor at Eagle Street, Holborn in London from 1804 to his death in 1834. He worked closely with Fuller on the committee of the BMS from 1812 and secretary of the Baptist Irish Society from 1814 to 1833. He was the author of many books, best known for his *History of the English Baptists* (4

Eagle Street, and Newman[4] of Stepney, I suppose, would be the editors. I saw Hinton.[5] He has been corresponding with the editors of the *Evangelical Magazine*, who, however, decline giving any explanation or correction of a paragraph which seemed to inculpate the Baptists as a denomination. He therefore withdraws from the *Evangelical Magazine*, and hopes the Baptists will do so with him.[6]

I saw Hughes[7] at the dinner of the Monthly Meeting. We sat next each other. He asked whether our translations were "without note or comment." I said I believed they were.

H[ughes]: "Do the translators make our own translation a sort of foundation, or do they translate directly from the originals?"

F[uller]: "I believe from the originals. They doubtless make use of our translation, and perhaps of others;

---

vols; 1811–1830). The standard biography is George Pritchard, *Memoir of the Life and Writings of the Rev. Joseph Ivimey* (London: George Wightman, 1835).

[4] William Newman (1773–1835) was pastor of the Baptist Church at Bow (1794–1811). He then became the first president of the Stepney Academy, later called Regent's Park College, until 1826. The standard biography is G. Pritchard, *Memoir of Rev. William Newman D.D.* (London: Thomas Ward & Co., 1837).

[5] James Hinton (1761–1823) pastor at the Baptist church in Oxford. Selections from his diary that reveal the Evangelical piety of Hinton are found in Chance Faulkner, ed., *The Diary of James Hinton* (Peterborough, ON: H&E Publishing, 2020).

[6] For more on the *Evangelical Magazine* controversy, see John Howard Hinton, *A Biographical Portraiture of the late Rev. James Hinton, M.A.* (Oxford: Bartlett and Hinton/London: B. J. Holdsworth, 1824), 305–307; Joseph Ivimey, *A History of the English Baptists comprising the principal events of the history of the Protestant Dissenters During the Reign of Geo III. And of the Baptist Churches in London* (London: Isaac Taylor, Hinton and Holdsworth & Ball, 1830), 4:117–120.

[7] Joseph Hughes (1769–1833) was for a time a tutor at the Bristol Baptist Academy, then the pastor of Battersea Baptist Church in London. He is best known for his work as one of the founders of the British and Foreign Baptist Society (BFBS) in 1804 and then serving as one of its secretaries. The standard biography of Hughes is John Leifchild, *Memoir of the Late Rev Joseph Hughes A.M.* (London: Thomas Ward And Co., 1835). The importance and significance of the work of the BFBS can be seen from Leslie Howsam, *Cheap Bibles: Nineteenth Century Publishing and the British and Foreign Bible Society* (Cambridge: Cambridge University Press, 1991).

1811

but no otherwise than as means of ascertaining the meaning of the originals."

H[ughes]: "How do they render the word βαπτίζω"

F[uller]: "In the Bengalee translation, and I suppose in all the others, by a word which signifies to immerse."

H[ughes]: "I think that is to be regretted."

F[uller]: "How then should they have done?"

H[ughes]: "As our translators have, left it untranslated, and only give the word a Bengalee termination."

F[uller]: "But why so?"

H[ughes]: "How else can Paedobaptists contribute towards its circulation?"

F[uller]: "If they would give a translation to any heathen nation, and render the word by a term that signifies to sprinkle, I would contribute to it; not on *that account*, but notwithstanding it."

H[ughes]: "I wish it had not been."

F[uller]: "Had they left the word untranslated, it would have been saying to the whole world either that they were not satisfied as to the meaning of it, which would be untrue, or that they had not given a faithful translation according to their best judgment, owing to the hope of patronage. I would not have had them act as you wish, Sir, for £20,000, nor, indeed, for any consideration."

He talked much about Catholicism, and in favour of translators being not Baptists or Paedobaptists, but more *literary men*. I answered that I disapproved of all union which required a sacrifice of principle; and as to his more literary men, they would not understand the Bible, and therefore could not do justice to it in a translation. I might have appealed to

Macknight,[8] and even to Campbell,[9] as examples; in whose hands, notwithstanding their great literary attainments, the spirit of the Scriptures evaporates. The edge, the unction, and the life of them are not found in their productions, which yet I should be sorry to be without.

I saw Sutcliff and Burls; we talked about the next London collection, the person to make it—could Christopher Anderson come? ... There is a talk among the denomination of a general *union*, and of an annual meeting in London. Could we not have our collection in April, and the sermons for our public collection on a week day, and so afford the opportunity for all who chose it, to attend without leaving their own places? Could not this service be accompanied with a communication of intelligence? Would not this be a *seed* out of which would grow insensibly the object wished for, a union of the denomination, and a union in an object worth uniting in—the promotion of the kingdom of Christ?

Now, you have quite a budget of the news of last week. You are, I suppose, what your countrymen call "a discreet man," and will make no improper use of it. Keep this letter, just as a diary of three days of your friend.

A. Fuller

---

[8] James MacKnight (1721-1800) was a Scottish minister and author of a number of theological books. He served at a number of churches that included Edinburgh Old Kirk from 1778-1800. He is best known for his book *Harmony of the Four Gospels* (London: William Strahan, 1756 [enlarged 2nd ed. 1763]). He was the Moderator of the General Assembly of the Church of Scotland in 1769.

[9] George Campbell (1719-1796) was a prominent Moderate scholar and Principal of Marischal College, Aberdeen (1759-1796); where he was also Professor of Divinity from 1771 to 1796. His many books including at least five editions of *Dissertation on Miracles* (Edinburgh: A. Kincaid & J. Bell, 1762); and *Translation of the Gospels*, first published in 1789; and six subsequent editions by 1834. See L.G. Kelly, "George Campbell's *Four Gospels* 1789" in Elizabeth A. Livingstone (ed.), *Studia Evangelica Vol VII: Papers presented to the Fifth International Congress on Biblical Studies 1973* (Berlin: Akademie Verlag, 1982), 277-282.

18
Mr. Anderson to Mr. Fuller[1]

February 1812
Liverpool

I received your journal of three days, a mark of friendship I truly value. Well, Hinton and the *Magazine*;[2] if you and Dr. Ryland[3] take part in it, do I entreat, let us have another *title*. The present is to me almost odious, at least I seldom hear the name of it pronounced by any who are not in our communion without almost blushing. This is not a little matter. The world is ruled by names; and it is a good pity if we most unwisely have bound a name to ourselves as a crown, which has been given us by our foes.[4] Had it been Christian, that worthy name by which our denomination had been most accurately described, how much better had it been for us. I am sure, my dear brother has, in the course of his life, thought not a little upon what is "lovely." Let us then wear a more inviting aspect. If a magazine should begin in London in the manner proposed, I regret that such circumstances should have given

---

[1] Anderson, *Life and Letters*, 198-200.
[2] *The Baptist Magazine* launched in 1809.
[3] John Ryland was appointed Minister of Broadmead Baptist Church, Bristol, and President of the Bristol Education Society (later called Bristol Baptist College) from 1793-1825. He was the son of John Collett Ryland, Minister of College Street Baptist Church, Northampton. The younger Ryland was assistant minister to his father for fifteen years prior to succeeding him as Minister in 1786, until his call to Bristol in 1793.
[4] Anderson from his own experience strongly believed that more effective work in Christian service could be accomplished when Christians unite across denominational boundaries in support of a common cause. See Talbot, *Search for a Common Identity*, 139-140, for more details.

birth to it, because without great care, much love and prudence, they will tinge, or in some way give a character to the publication. It would be very gratifying if, on the contrary, it should draw forth both fear and love, and continue to display a truly Christian spirit. ... I am persuaded the religious intelligence department might be of great service. Besides, considering the missionary aspect which the denomination is supposed to wear, an interesting and well-arranged communication of intelligence is no more than ought to be expected. ... Indeed I feel truly anxious, that with our principles we could assume that sedate and steadfast, yet lovely and amiable appearance, which belonged to ancient Christianity. Oh that the Church of God had recovered her long lost gentleness and unity![5]

But everything valuable has its counterfeit. I hope I shall be preserved from the latitudinarianism of some. I think I have yet to be instructed in the logic of Brother Hughes. He is treading on slippery ground, and, with his views, seems to me in great danger of being allured away and losing himself. What cause of gratitude have we that God has been pleased to preserve our literary men! Surely there can be no charm in the walls of a college. What does Brother Hughes mean? Where is the scholar? What is the linguist? Where are the literary men of this age? Methinks God has made foolish the wisdom of this age.[6] Within these few years enough has been done by a few men, who, to this day it should seem, are, by courtesy, permitted to be literary—enough to put the rest to silence and

---

[5] From the 1790s to around 1830 there was a remarkable degree of co-operation in a variety of mission initiatives between Protestant Church leaders in the United Kingdom. See R.H. Martin, *Evangelicals United: Ecumenical Stirrings in Pre-Victorian Britain, 1795-1830* (Metuchen, NJ: The Scarecrows Press, 1983).

[6] See 1 Corinthians 1:20.

1812

to shame; or at least as much as to show the importance and beauty of learning being blended with humility and piety. I am far from despising what he is talking of so often and so bigly; yet, humanly speaking, how little would to this day have been effected, if our brethren had not possessed piety, eminent piety.

About the London collection: I wish you could improve upon it. Owing to this Liverpool visit, I am bereaved of the pleasure of serving my beloved brethren in the East in this—yet I never decline this service without a struggle. Is there no possibility of the collection being got on another plan? ... I mean some plan which would leave the minister more time for study and spiritual conversion—which would not so dissipate the mind—which would keep him a *little* more in his own sphere. If I have time previously to arrange, I can manage, yet not with so much comfort to myself in the pulpit, or with such advantage to others. I like your manner of meeting annually, better than that of calling for a religious mob, and can as yet see no great good from what Rowland Hill[7] calls the "Religious Washing Week," with which he is annually almost overset. A multitude of ministers brought together in a hasty manner is not at all an advisable measure. I wish they may relinquish it.

I long very much occasionally to be with you. The Redeemer prepares completely the mansions of his people; but it

---

[7] Rowland Hill (1744-1833) was an Anglican clergyman of independent means. He built the well-known Surrey Chapel, Blackfriars Road, London, for his own ministry where services were conducted with Anglican forms of worship. He had an effective open-air ministry and engaged in lengthy preaching tours. His church had a most effective work amongst children with thirteen Sunday Schools attached to it. He helped to found the Religious Tract Society, the British and Foreign Bible Society, and the London Missionary Society. The standard biography is William Jones, *Memoir of the Rev Rowland Hill M.A.* (London: Henry G. Bohn, 1845).

is not inconsistent with love to him, that the departure of his children should render heaven more desirable, and, in a subordinate sense, prepare their way. I am sure if you should go before me, I shall include you in my ideas of future enjoyment, as I now do the names of Pearce[8] and others.

Your ever affectionate brother,

Christ[topher] Anderson

---

[8] Samuel Pearce (1766–1799).

19
Mr. Fuller to Mr. Anderson[1]

May 4, 1812
Kettering

My dear brother,

Some time ago I expressed to you some thoughts which had been in my mind respecting your being my successor in the Secretary-ship of the India Mission, but which, from other occurrences, I had then relinquished. The continuance of my inward complaints and the consequent decrease of my wonted energies, have forced the subject anew on my mind, and not my mind only; my brethren in the Mission begin to consider my labours as drawing to a close, and discover anxiety about a successor. A recent conversation on the subject with three of them (Hinton, Burls, and Sutcliff), has left a serious impression on my mind, not of dejection, but of concern for the work which is every year increasing in importance. They say, "You must have an assistant, and that not only as a pastor, but as a secretary, who, by being introduced to the work, shall be able to carry on when you are laid aside." I mentioned the difficulty in finding a suitable person; your name was mentioned as one whose heart was in the work, and whose hand was ready with the pen, &c; but is it lawful to ask him to leave his present station? Is he not already in a great sphere of active labour?

---

[1] Anderson, *Life and Letters*, 200-202.

Answer: he is; but there are men in Scotland who can do his work whereas there seems none equally suited for this. Is it lawful to remove from a sphere of useful labour, and dissolve the pastoral relation? Certainly not on light occasions; but if none, Carey,[2] had been still at Leicester, or rather at Moulton.

My dear brother, I do not ask for a speedy answer to so serious a question, but merely submit it for your consideration, and that, without mentioning a word of it to anyone, you may make it a matter of prayer and reflection. You know the real importance of the object—an object, too, but for which it is doubtful whether you had gone into the ministry. You know the turning of events by which you were prevented from going abroad; perhaps for the very purpose of serving the object at home. You know the cordiality with which your labours are regarded, not only at Kettering,[3] but amongst all our brethren. Consider whether those things have not a voice in them—whether your post might not be filled by some other brother, &c. Should I be removed, and you succeed me as pastor of the Church (which would be very gratifying to me), you would then receive what now supports me; and meanwhile, I should wish you not to be a mere assistant but a co-pastor, and the Society would allow you sufficient, I believe, to satisfy you. Indeed, they might very well afford this, not only as having no other officer to pay, but as, while we both lived and were able to work, we should more than cover it by the extra collections that would be made for the Mission.

---

[2] William Carey, prior to service in India had served as the pastor of Moulton Baptist Church, Northamptonshire (1785-1789), until his call to Harvey Lane Baptist Church, Leicester, where he stayed until his departure for India in June 1793.

[3] Kettering Baptist Church.

1812

Say nothing of the subject at present to anyone, nor convey any hint of my ill state of health. It is true, I continue to preach, but often with much difficulty. I lose flesh and spirits, and have such a susceptibility of cold as to be always in danger. When I cannot get sleep, fever preys upon my frame. It is now more than a year since these complaints have been upon me. Journeys, if I could have a warm and dry air, do me good, and have engaged Mr. John Hall[4] to assist me till the end of the year, I hope this summer to go several excursions.

My kinsman, Joseph Fuller, whom I baptised a few years since, a youth of great promise, died on the 25th March, of consumption.

Though I have requested you to say nothing on the above subject, yet if you wish to write to me upon it, do so.—I am, &c,

A. Fuller

---

[4] John Keen Hall was appointed assistant to Andrew Fuller in Kettering Baptist Church (later called Fuller Baptist Church) in 1812 and succeeded him as the pastor after Fuller's death on Sunday May 7, 1815. Keen continued as pastor until his own death in 1829 aged 43. For more details on the history of this church see Ashley and Jenny Butlin, *Fuller Baptist Church—An Outline History 1696-1991*.

20
Mr. Anderson to Mr. Fuller[1]

May 23, 1812
Edinburgh

My ever dear brother,

Although I have made no reply to your last, and, as it respects myself, important letter, you will not suppose that I have been indifferent to it. No, it has bowed my spirits in a degree ever since, and made me look round on my various present engagements with feelings unknown before.

I am still unable to send you a reply, and you will not wonder at this. I mean such a reply as you might wish, containing reasons for or against. I seem as though I never would get beyond the threshold. When I sit down, my incompetency presents itself uniformly, if not insistently, or if not at first, it returns upon me, so that I am prevented from beginning to think of other matters upon which (I must be ingenuous) my heart recoils. I hope that our blessed Lord will, in his mercy, interpose and guide my path for his glory, though at present I cannot help thinking that even you, my brother, would be almost afraid of calling me from my present situation, when once you hear of all circumstances.

Though at present I see not the possibility of my removal to lend my poor assistance, yet the state of my beloved brother's health, and his mind in regard to the dear object of our mutual cause, has occupied no small portion of my thoughts

---

[1] Anderson, *Life and Letters*, 202–204.

since I heard of them. Matters appear, in your own apprehension, to be in such a state as to call for some speedy arrangement, and when I saw the note in the *Evangelical*, advertising your preaching in June, I wished occasionally, for the sake of the Mission and my own soul, that I could be with you, to pray and ponder over the path of duty. This, however, appears to me impracticable. ... You have any prospect of being nearer to Edinburgh this year any time then when you are at home? My chief reason for wishing to see you, would be to talk over the whole of this business, and to consult whether there could not be some extension of your plan as to home management. ... You have precluded me very properly from saying a word to anyone. Neither would I. It is a subject so delicate, each is now my place as the affections of a few, that it would have excited unnecessary, because premature, grief and concern. I hope I could rely on the serious and impartial consideration of the Church of God. I am, I trust, at the disposal of his people, provided they act with prayer and deliberation. From the success which has attended my feeble efforts, and my having been, accustomed to observe, as I thought, the hand of God is many circumstances, since I began here, I must feel a peculiar impression as to its being the place where the Saviour intended me to settle.

For several years past I have had too much to do beside the Church. It's being small probably led me to seek round sufficient work to occupy me; but as it has increased as well as the other, I find myself behind occasionally with my engagements, which gives me considerable uneasiness. Oh! For light from above, that we might say in this matter, "Come. then, and let us walk in the light of the Lord."[2] I pray for your

---

[2] See Isaiah 2:5.

health in body and soul, and am, my dear brother, with sincere attachment, &c.

Christ[opher] Anderson

21
Mr. Anderson to Mr. Fuller[1]

June 22, 1812
Edinburgh

... In my last I spoke of inability, and that I cannot well get over. To be ingenuous, some parts of your present employments I might accomplish; perhaps constitutionally, and in some respects, I may be fitted for them, but there are other parts where I must fail, I fear, so as far as to endanger the success of the whole, e.g., preaching, &c. Granting, however, that all this were overruled, I would now say, I am, I trust, the servant of the Lord, and upon the general question feel ready to act for him. I would desire to have no will of my own, nor allow any feelings to interpose and prevent from acting as I ought disinterestedly. But as yet I have been quite unable to discover the path of duty. At such a time as this, you will not consider the following account in ostentation, nor would I write so to any one, except there was a sufficient call for it.

You know that a very considerable share of the business, and often the prosperity of institutions, depends upon those with whom they originated.

Now it so happens that I should have been in a considerable degree so favoured with regard to the Itinerant Society,[2]

---

[1] Anderson, *Life and Letters*, 204-206.

the Edinburgh Bible Society,³ and the Gaelic School Society.⁴ With respect to the first, I might perhaps as effectually promote it in England. As to the second, though at present almost the whole depends upon me, yet a successor could be found; but it would as yet no easy matter to find one for the last; at least I think so, according to the manner in which the institution should be carried on, or rather fully established. All the above, however, are infant causes, and if you allow me to add, they require, especially the last, all the enthusiasm of the original projectors to carry these through at present. In Edinburgh you are to know regularly that in the midst of, I hope, much good, there is a large share of indifference in many Christians, and of indisposition to go out of the way for Christ. Persons disposed, therefore, to take these offices are by no means easy to be found.

---

² The Scotch Itinerant Society (SIS) was the Baptist home mission body in Scotland set up by George Barclay and Christopher Anderson in 1808. Andrew Fuller had urged the English body promoting similar work in England to grant some initial funding to help launch this venture in its first few years. See Talbot, *Search for a Common Identity*, 154-156, for more details. Details of the exertions of one of the SIS's most effective evangelists is found in: D. Sinclair, *Journal of Itinerating Exertions in some of the more destitute parts of Scotland* (6 Vols; Edinburgh: Andrew Balfour, 1816).

³ Details of the formation and early work of the Edinburgh Bible Society is found in G.A Frank Knight, D.D., "The History of The National Bible Society of Scotland, Part I 1809-1900," (typescript MS, n.d.), 9-14; and William C. Somerville, *From Iona to Dunblane* (Edinburgh: National Bible Society of Scotland, 1948), 12-17.

⁴ The Welsh-language travelling schools of Griffith John and Thomas Charles, inspired Christopher Anderson, together with some likeminded colleagues from various Protestant denominations, to establish the Edinburgh Society for the Support off Gaelic Schools in November 1810. Similar societies promoting this cause were established in Glasgow (1812) and Inverness (1818). For more details on the Gaelic Schools Society, see Anderson, *Life and Letters of Christopher Anderson*, 125-134; Donald E. Meek, "Christopher Anderson, The Scottish Highlands and Ireland," in Donald E. Meek (ed.), *A Mind For Mission: Essays in Appreciation of The Rev. Christopher Anderson (1782-1852)* (Edinburgh: Scottish Baptist History Project, 1992), 17-24; and D.E. Meek, "Gaelic School Societies," in Cameron, ed., *Dictionary of Scottish Church History and Theology*, 349-350.

1812

My greatest difficulty remains—the church at Richmond Court. With me also this attempt originated, and it has, blessed be God, so far succeeded, and I feel assured will do so if properly conducted. You will not, my dear brother, wonder that I should add, that when I reflect on the degree of success with which the Lord has been most graciously pleased to crown these measures, I am almost afraid to think of removing—afraid lest I should offend the Lord in a situation to which his finger seems directly pointing.

Have you invariably thought of dwelling at Kettering essentially necessary to the business of the Mission being partially attempted by another, and that the colleague in the one should be so in the Church? Could he who undertakes mission business not be settled anywhere else, and at same time assist you? Even on the supposition of my not remaining all my life at Edinburgh, I have always meditated being elsewhere as I did here. I still possess some feature of a missionary, and am decidedly partial to raising a new interest, as you call it in England. The difficulties and discouragements in the morning of such an enterprise, however strange it may seem to some, are pleasing to me. Its infant concerns are my delight. Then, though you may think me childish, I must add, since I was a boy, having been accustomed to live in the midst of a pretty numerous society, a city life, or one in the vicinity, has become so congenial to me that it seems needful to keep me to my work. I am very fond of the country and of nature, but there I should be strongly tempted to inactivity, though I had much to do. I leave you then, my dear brother, to determine on the following proposal. It is nothing short of my coming to see you, or of our meeting together somewhere, if the Lord will. Many things I could then state which cannot be commu-

nicated, or at least settled by epistolary correspondence. ...
Ever yours in much love, &c.,

Christ[topher] Anderson

22
Mr. Fuller to Mr. Anderson[1]

July 2, 1812
Kettering

My dear brother,

I received both your letters, and should have answered ere now, but could not till now be certain as to a journey in which I could propose to meet you. I think, from your last especially, I cannot press the object; yet I should wish to see you. I am engaged to preach and collect for the Mission at Nottingham on the 12th instant. On Tuesday the 14th, I shall be at Derby, at Mr. Smith's,[2] the Baptist minister. If you could reach that place by Wednesday the 15th, it would do, as I shall stop there over Wednesday night. Brother Ryland is with me and unites in love.

---

[1] Anderson, *Life and Letters*, 206-207.

[2] This is Rev. William Smith, minister of Agard Street Particular Baptist Church, Derby, from 1805-1812. We are thankful to Julian Locke, Regent's Park College, Oxford, for identifying this individual. For more details on this church see Stephen Greasley, *The Baptists of Derbyshire 1650-1914* (Ilkeston: Moorley's Print & Publishing, 2007), 180-181. Smith had previously served in Claremont Baptist Church, Shrewsbury, from 1783-1789. See Michael J. Collis, *An Account of the Baptist Churches of Shropshire and the surrounding Areas* (Newtown: Shropshire Group of Baptist Churches, 2008), 69, 86, 97.

23
Mr. Anderson to Mr. Fuller[1]

September 23, 1812
Edinburgh

My beloved brother,

Yesterday week Dr. Marshman[2] spread the book of Providence before us, and since that time, mysterious and melancholy as the tidings were, I have been reading it with wonder and praise. Having advertised a collection at Richmond Court for Sabbath evening, I preached from "O the depth of the riches," &c. (Rom. 11:33-35). ... At the conclusion, I remarked that money would be got. I had no doubt of this. I only wished, for certain reason, that it might be got soon; for the truth is, we have an instrument in our hands at present which we never had before. If the desolation is removed and repaired quickly, there is no saying what will be the effect. The wall of Jerusalem is raised up amid much opposition and many discouragements, but it was finished in fifty-two days. "And it came to pass that when all our enemies heard thereof, and all the heathen that were about us saw these things, they were much cast down in their own eyes; for they perceived that this work was wrought of our God!"[3]

Pardon this long digression. We have got £55 pounds last Sabbath, but collect again next. On Monday, at our Commit-

---

[1] Anderson, *Life and Letters*, 210-211.
[2] Joshua Marshman BMS Missionary in Bengal 1799-1837, news of the fire at Serampore on March 11, 1812.
[3] Nehemiah 6:16.

tee Meeting of the Edinburgh Bible Society, we had £279 in the bank; we voted £300, trusting to God; and in the same evening a sum of £43 came in, the produce of the first quarter of our penny-a-week Societies in Edinburgh, so that our patience was not long tried. I had a letter, by return of post, from Brother Burnett, with £50; and we are going on receiving sums of £10 and £5 from various persons. The Doctor[4] has got about £80 or £90; C.A.[5] about £160, besides the £300 as above. I hope Edinburgh will produce £800 or £1000. Such is the place which our dear brethren hold in the affections and esteem of all cases. After all, however, this is a severe stroke. God grant it maybe sanctifies to us, and great good will come out of it, and before long you may preach again from "O sing a new song to the Lord, for His right hand and holy arm has gotten him the victory!"[6] Excuse this hurried scrawl I intended to merely show that it is in my heart to live and die with you.—Yours &c.

Christ[topher] Anderson

---

[4] Charles Stuart.
[5] Christopher Anderson, the author of this letter.
[6] Psalm 98:1.

24
Mr. Fuller to Mr. Anderson[1]

September 27, 1812
Kettering

I have been out a month in Norfolk. You heard of this fire before I did, which was not till the 18th.[2] At Norwich I had collected about £200, and left it; but on the news reaching Mark Wilks,[3] he went to work again, and on the first day got 100 guineas. ... I learn that the London ministers mean to collect in London, and give us a collection in each of their congregations. I should not wonder if the wall were built in "fifty-two days." Thank you and your friends for all your love and zeal.

Write by all means to Marshman and Ward.[4] They know you.

15 October. I wish and hope the subscriptions towards the loss will be in No. 23, *Periodical Accounts*. If they can be got together in the time you have marked out, fifty-two days, they may be inserted.

---

[1] Anderson, *Life and Letters*, 211-213

[2] In March 1812 a devastating fire destroyed both property and some of the most precious manuscripts on which William Carey had been working in Serampore, together with a large collection of type founts and paper. See Stanley, *History of the Baptist Missionary Society*, 38, 56.

[3] Mark Wilks (1748-1819) was the minister of St Clements Baptist Church, Norwich (later known as Wheeler's Chapel), 1788-1819. He was also viewed as a radical in his political views, for example concerning the French Revolution. See C.B. Jewson, "Norwich Baptists and the French Revolution," *Baptist Quarterly* 24, No. 5, (January, 1972): 209-215. The standard biography of Wilks is Sarah Wilks, *Memoirs of Rev. Mark Wilks, late of Norwich* (London: Francis Westley, 1821).

[4] William Carey's longstanding colleagues Joshua Marshman and William Ward.

30 October. I think your allusion to Neh. 6:15, 16, will be verified. Some of our friends in London think it is so, or that the loss is already repaired. I think this is rather too much, but it will be so very soon. The London subscription is £1500.

9 November. I have just looked over yours, and am much inclined to adopt your advice respecting Nos. 23 and 24, *P[eriodical] A[ccounts].* Coming home this morning I found a letter from Mr. Mardon,[5] Goamalty,[6] who has extracted an account of the Serampore fire from the "Asiatic Mirror," a Calcutta newspaper, of March 25. After enumerating the particulars of the loss, they add,

> From the above sketch, our readers may form some idea of the direction and extent of the labours of the Oriental missionary press, and how much the public at large, and the friends of literature in particular, have cause to regret the accident which has interrupted its useful career; but we trust that the interruption will prove short in duration, and limited in its effort. ... We confidently trust that their printing establishment will, like the Phoenix of antiquity, rise from its ashes winged with new strength, and destined in a lofty and long-enduring flight, widely to diffuse the benefits of knowledge throughout the East.

---

[5] [Richard] Mardon and Mrs. Mardon, British BMS missionaries, together with Kristna Dass and several other Indian converts were formed into a church in Goamalty in 1808. Marton was stationed here to superintend the Bengalee schools which had previously been set up by mission workers. Kristna was engaged in evangelistic work and distributed large quantities of Bibles and Christian gospel tracts among the local population. Information obtained on September 13, 2022 from https://www.wmcarey.edu/carey/missgaz/stations.htm. See also Stanley, *History of the Baptist Missionary Society*, 43.

[6] The town of Goamalty was near the ancient city of Gour, formerly the capital of Bengal, between Cutwa and Dinagepore, about 200 miles north of Calcutta [now known as Kolkata today]. Information obtained on September 13, 2022 from https://www.wmcarey.edu/carey/missgaz/stations.htm.

1813

If my conjecture be right, this article was inserted by some such friend as [J.H.] Harrington,[7] Esq., President of the Calcutta Auxiliary Bible Society, who, I know, was so interested in the business, as to take the statement of the loss to the Governor-General, and to propose to his Lordship a subscription in the city towards repairing it, to which his Lordship cheerfully consented—but the whole was stopped by a suggestion that they did not need it, ... from a quarter that would not, after so much professed "sympathy," have been suspected.

Money is coming from various quarters. The Mission was never more prosperous. It is cheering to think of the interest that is felt for it by Christians of all denominations. We have thought the Christians of the South to have done wonders, but you of the North keep ahead of us. Make our grateful acknowledgments to the members of your Bible Society, and to all others who have come forward on this occasion.

A. Fuller

---

[7] John Herbert Harington (1765-1828) was an Anglican Christian. He was recognised as a British orientalist, colonial administrator and judge in Calcutta. See Rigg, James McMullen, "Harington, John Herbert," *Dictionary of National Biography* (London: Smith, Elder & Co, 1885-1900), 24:389-390 for more information on his life.

25
Mr. Anderson to Mr. Fuller[1]

February 6, 1813
Edinburgh

... Well, I have read No. 23[2] with peculiar pleasure. My heart goes along with every paragraph of your letter to the churches. But why so much, my dear brother, of the dying swan-song in it? It leaves a somber impression, and perhaps you meant it to do so, but I hope the Lord will yet spare you to us for many days.[3] It is, however, a fine state of mind, that of anticipating our eternal rest as the end of all our wanderings, and all the toils here below. O what interest there is to my mind, in the idea of heaven being the rendezvous of all the "taught of God"[4] and Jesus in the midst! What a "gathering together unto him"[5] that will be. Though, however, you may think of sitting and singing yourself away to glory, perhaps to abide in the flesh is the will of Jesus still; and if so, I for one shall truly

---

[1] Anderson, *Life and Letters*, 214.

[2] "Periodic Accounts of the BMS Mission in India" No XXIII, bound in *Periodical Accounts Relative to the Baptist Missionary Society*, 4:319-496.

[3] This written report is generally encouraging with respect to the progress of the work in India. It is likely that Anderson is referring to page 458 and Fuller's comments that several of the earlier supporters of BMS are probably not going to be alive much longer. It is probable that Fuller is concerned that London Baptists will try and take over the mission when he and others have died and remove it from the control of the Association where it began. He was correct in discerning some difficult years ahead concerning the future of the mission and the strained relations that would develop between the Serampore pioneers and some of the younger generation of BMS leaders in London. See "Contending for the Ark: The Succession to Andrew Fuller" in Stanley, *History of the Baptist Missionary Society*, 29-35.

[4] Isaiah 54:13; John 6:45.

[5] 2 Thessalonians 2:1-2.

rejoice. It was after I had read your letter some days, that I was charmed with a clause about David: "Now, behold, *in my trouble*, I have prepared for the house ... one hundred thousand talents of gold, ... so David prepared abundantly *before his death*."[6] And so you say you have been providing for futurity, by the including of a few younger brethren in the committee. God grant that at what time they are, in the providence of the Lord, called out to his assistance, they may prove themselves men. May they indeed be gold and silver, and precious stones; this would indeed prove "gold for the things of gold, and silver for the things of silver."[7] Excuse this familiar way of filling my sheet. My kind respects to Mr. Hall,[8] if at Kettering.

I am, my dear Brother, yours with inviolable and unfading affection,

Christ[opher] Anderson

---

[6] 1 Chronicles 22:14, 5.
[7] 1 Chronicles 19:2.
[8] Robert Hall Jr.

26
Mr. Fuller to Mr. Anderson[1]

February 21, 1813
Kettering

I sent the *Periodical Accounts* to you through Dr. S[tuart] and I do the same with these. I think everything should be done in such a manner as to give an old man, who has greatly interested himself the mission, every mark of respect, and even of precedence. Let him do all he wishes without oppressing him, just as he has done before.

I have been thinking of late of the force of this petition: "Take not thy Holy Spirit from me."[2] As spiritual things are spiritually discerned, if the Lord leave us to ourselves we shall lose sight of the gospel, and somehow get beside it. I have heard many ingenious sermons, and perhaps have preached some, in which the gospel was overlooked; and if a sinner had heard it, and never heard the way of salvation before, he might have died, and gone to the bar of God, for anything he could have heard then, without having been told his danger, or the way of salvation! Take not thy Holy Spirit from us! It is for want of spirituality of mind, surely, that there is so much orthodox, and at the same time so little evangelical preaching.

I am dear Brother, affectionately yours,

A. Fuller

---

[1] Anderson, *Life and Letters*, 214–215.
[2] Psalm 51:11.

27
Mr. Anderson to Mr. Fuller[1]

February 27, 1813
Edinburgh

My dear brother,

I regret much that I have not fulfilled my promise. I was under the necessity of leaving home for the west of Scotland, which really put it out of my power, and this week I have been almost worn out with my engagements. They thicken around me, and it seems as though I most do what I can to fulfil my work. I felt what you said to Brother D.[2] about the danger of neglecting one's own vineyard, nay, and one's own soul, amid various other engagements, all good and all beautiful in their season. My own situation is, in many respects, all I could wish; but there is a wheel within a wheel, and my own individual circumstances become increasingly mysterious.

You seem afraid that I should act without modesty and tenderness towards our good old friend Dr. S[tuart]. I really do what I can, and I hear no complaints from this quarter. I now more and more desire to live peaceably with *all* men.[3] Assure yourself that I am polite towards the good man; that though I cannot come into all his views, he seems to love me with all my faults, and I love, and often pity him with all his.

---

[1] Anderson, *Life and Letters*, 215-216.
[2] The identity of this person is uncertain. One possibility is that it might be a prominent Glasgow Baptist layman James Deakin, treasurer of the Glasgow Auxiliary Society to BMS, who was well known to both Fuller and Anderson. See Talbot, *Search for a Common Identity*, 138
[3] Romans 12:8.

He is getting old indeed, and I would be far from doing anything to disturb him in the least. ... You, I am sure, do not wish to shed a tear over me as ruined by strange and mistaken scrupulosity of conscience in regard to a thousand things, about which many good people here are always perplexing themselves, and endeavouring to perplex others. Oh that I may be enabled to do justly, to love mercy, and to walk humbly with my God.[4] I am much impressed of late years with my remaining impurity. More and more do I breathe after heaven as a state of purity, as well as a place of happiness.

I am, dear brother, affectionately yours,

Christ[topher] Anderson

---

[4] Micah 6:8.

28
Mr. Anderson to Mr. Fuller[1]

April 2, 1813
Edinburgh

I thank you for your favour of yesterday, which our friend the Doctor[2] has read. It was read yesterday in the side-room, where our petition is being signed, and will be read in our Committee this evening.[3] In your letter you give me the draft of a petition for various towns and cities. I must, in reply, tell you a story. In the year 1797, a number of cities and counties in this kingdom abhorring the principle, and feeling the effects of the war, and disapproving of the measures of those by whom it was conducted, petitioned the King, as a pre-requisite to the restoration of peace, to dismiss his ministers. The petitioners having the same object in view, happened to express their wishes in nearly the same language. The supporters of the Ministry on this very account, insisted that all

---

[1] Anderson, *Life and Letters*, 216-218.
[2] Charles Stuart.
[3] The East India Company had recently (1812 or early 1813) imposed some restrictions on the preaching of the gospel to the native population in Bengal and had created further obstacles in the way of Christian missionaries entering or remaining in the country. It was a difficult time for BMS as some of the affected missionaries were sailing to India at the time the restrictions were put in place. See Anderson, *Life of Christopher Anderson*, 216. In 1813, considerable pressure was put on the company through petitions raised by Evangelical Protestants for greater freedom for missionary work in India. For more details on the policies of the Company and the petitions against it, see Karen Chancey, "The Star in the East: The Controversy over Christian Missions to India, 1805-1813," *The Historian* 60, No.3 (Spring 1998): 507-522; and Penelope Carson, *The East India Company and Religion, 1698-1858* (Woodbridge, Suffolk: Boydell & Brewer, 2012).

the petitions must have been fabricated in the same mint; and as the Duke of Bedford had taken the lead in the Westminster petition, they asserted them all to be his production.

I had this story from no one here. I believe it to be correct, and you will make what use of it you think proper in your future movements. But as you, the Secretary, are a marked man on this occasion, at least by the President of the Board of Control, your language may be observed. Now, if your form is adopted by other towns, I would strongly recommend to your consideration the propriety of the Kettering petition being different.

We had from Dr. Campbell,[4] on Monday, a most interesting, noble, argumentative, and feeling speech, in the course of which he gave us a short detail of what had been done in India. It was, indeed, one of the finest testimonies for God and his Christ that I ever heard in a promiscuous meeting. In the picture there stood Brother Carey in the foreground, clothed in the insignia of his office, and I could suppose him blushing, and anxious to hide his head in a corner. I must say, however, that he simply got what was his due, and there was, I assure you, none of that blending of his labours with those of other men or bodies of men. When disapproving of the disposition shown by the East India Company, and of the spirit beginning to show itself on the part of Government to symbolize with them in this matter, he said,

---

[4] Dr Campbell was a Church of Scotland minister in that city, according to Anderson, *Life and Letters*, 217. It is probably John Campbell (1758–1828), who in 1805 was appointed the last minister of the second charge of the Tolbooth, Edinburgh. (That is, one of the four parishes contained within the subdivided St. Giles Cathedral). He was also appointed as the secretary of the Society for Propagating Christian Knowledge in Scotland in 1806 and Moderator of the General Assembly of the Church of Scotland in 1818. His doctorate awarded in 1807 was an honorary one from Edinburgh University. See also A. Ian Dunlop, *The Kirks of Edinburgh 1560-1984* (Edinburgh: Scottish Records Society New Series 15 & 16, 1989), 98.

1813

And are we now arrived at a period, my lord, when any Government shall rise up and say, "The Kingdom of Christ shall not come?" I have heard of a Government which, by its executive members, rose up and said, "That there is no God, and that death is an eternal sleep;" but I never heard that even that Government said, "You shall not propagate your sentiments upon these subjects."

I may only add, that you will give us as early intimation as possible of your journey to Scotland this year. Is your meeting at Northampton or Kettering considered as the annual one of the Baptist Missionary Society? Oh let us never be moved away from the unostentatious and yet ardent and effectual mode of procedure. You know that I am yours, &c.

29
Mr. Fuller to Mr. Anderson[1]

May 25, 1813
Kettering

... Respecting my visit, I have exchanged a letter or two on a very tender subject, and in a very tender way, with Mr. G.E. of Glasgow,[2] and have promised him to be in Scotland, God willing, in July, and to make his house, as heretofore, my home. Such, it appeared to me, after what passed between us, was my duty. I think of setting off on Monday, June 28, to be in Edinburgh by Saturday, July 4. I should like to go and see good Mr. Stewart of Dingwall,[3] if it were possible, and if you can so arrange my journey, do so.

3rd June. The above plan must be a little changed. I had better be a week later at Edinburgh than I proposed. *The Brief Narrative* is in want of the maps. Prey hasten them as much as possible, and send them to Ivimey,[4] or Burls.[5]

---

[1] Anderson, *Life and Letters*, 218.

[2] Greville Ewing.

[3] Alexander Stewart (1764-1821) was a noted Gaelic scholar and Evangelical Church of Scotland minister. His first charge was in Moulin, Perthshire from 1786 to 1805; then in Dingwall, north of Inverness, 1805-1820; and Canongate, Edinburgh, 1820-1821. See D.E. Meek, "Stewart, Alexander (1764-1821)" in Cameron, ed., *Scottish Church History and Theology*, 792-793. A biography written on him is J. Sievewright, *Memoirs of the Late Alexander Stewart* (Edinburgh: 1882).

[4] Joseph Ivimey (1773-1834) was the pastor of Eagle Street Baptist church in London, and an important English Particular Baptist historian. He was also the first secretary for the Baptist Society for Promoting the Gospel in Ireland.

[5] William Burls (1763-1837) was a merchant and served as deacon at Carter Lane Baptist Church in London.

30
Mr. Anderson to Mr. Fuller[1]

June 9, 1813
Edinburgh

Dr. Stuart and I agree in thinking, that as you go this time to Inverness, it would be by much the best plan to take the West of Scotland first, and return home by Edinburgh. I shall give a sketch of the tour which we propose. ... I must here, however, notice that you never have visited several large towns in the South of Scotland, as Peebles, Kelso, Jelburgh, Selkirk, &c. Now these, if you regard the necessity for a stranger's voice being heard in them proclaiming the unsearchable riches of Christ, really demand a visit. Not but that the gospel is preached, but those who do so need a second witness; and besides, it might tend to interest a very considerable body of respectable people in the Mission, and, of course, might be of infinite importance to their own souls. Dr. Stuart is intent upon this part of the journey. Agree, therefore, my esteemed brother, to the eight Sabbaths, and all will immediately be advertised. In regard to your companion, could Brother Hall of Leicester not come? Dr. Stuart says he would make a noise at least, and I believe, do much more. You know that Brother Sutcliff is beloved in Scotland—I should be happy were it possible for him to travel with you up the Highland road. If this cannot be, you know the Scotch taste.

I am ever, with esteem, yours unfeignedly,

Christ[opher] Anderson

---

[1] Anderson, *Life and Letters*, 218-219.

31
Mr. Fuller to Mr. Anderson[1]

June 14, 1813
Kettering

My dear brother,

You and Dr. Stuart seem to think this the last time of my visiting Scotland, and therefore are for making the most of it. If you do not, however, I do. But I never knew such a year of toil before as this has hitherto been. This petitioning, writing to and waiting on the Members of Parliament, which required three and four journeys to London—the removing and setting up of my two eldest children in business in Kettering—although I am overset. The way in which this sometimes operates is a violent attack of the bile. This I have had this week, and I am now under medical control, and unable to preach tomorrow. These and other attacks cause "fears to be in the way," when great journeys and labours are before me. There is another thing that lies heavier upon my heart about leaving home than the above, which is the state of the Church at Kettering. In watching the India vineyard, my friends often tell me I neglect my own; and I cannot disprove this charge. Four or five Lord's-days is all that I have been used to allow beyond the Tweed. I suppose you ask for eight, as dealers do who mean to abate, thinking I could not offer less than six. Well, I do think of six, but cannot think of any more, and for this I must put off the North of England to another year. ... As to

---

[1] Anderson, *Life and Letters*, 219-220.

R[obert] Hall, he is now in Kettering, and preached last week at the Association. I mentioned what you said last night, but the prejudices conceived against him by some, where he must visit, of which he knows, have produced a reaction.[2] If he were able he would not come; but he is not able, on account of complaints of long standing. He is prejudiced rather in favour of Scotland in general. His sermons are unusually solemn and impressive; days and months can scarcely efface the impression which they leave, not of words, but things. I think him much more spiritual, humble, and unaffected, than many of my acquaintance, and who are godly men too.

Affectionately yours, &c,

A. Fuller

---

[2] See Anderson, *Life and Letters*, 184 n., 220 n.

32
Mr. Anderson to Mr. Fuller[1]

December 1, 1813
Edinburgh

My beloved brother,

Both your letters I duly received. ... It seems strange that I have not written to you since we parted. Assuredly it is not because I did not value and much enjoy your last visit. I was glad, because I fondly hoped it seemed the will of Providence that you should abide with me yet for a good while to come. But what a world is this in which we now live! Is it indeed the world into which we were born? What times have passed over all the kingdoms of the countries in the short space which has elapsed since we were singing Dr. Watt's 117th Psalm,[2] to the tune of Eaton, in the chaise in the north, and much less than this. The cities of the nation have fallen, indeed! Every capital in Europe, except London, Stockholm, and Constantinople. Nor is it unworthy of our notice, that wherever the destroyer of these cities has gone beyond a certain line, he has failed; and that line is the boundary of what has been considered as the seat of the Beast. He went to Palestine, to Egypt, but he was beyond the line, and he must return. He went to Moscow,

---

[1] Anderson, *Life and Letters*, 223-224.

[2] Isaac Watts (1674-1748) was a prominent English Congregational minister, theologian and hymn-writer. Further information on the significance of Watts can be obtained from David Fountain, *Isaac Watts 1674-1748 Remembered* (Southampton: Mayflower Publications, 1974); and G. Beynon, *Isaac Watts His Life and Thought* (Tain: Christian Focus, 2013). A more recent study of Watts theological convictions is G. Beynon, *Isaac Watts: Reason, Passion and the Revival of Religion* (Edinburgh: T. & T. Clark, 2016).

the capital still of Russia, he was beyond the line, and it should seem he has been upon the decline since, and even before it. Madrid and Lisbon being once entered and humbled, the tide turned, as they were the last. Stockholm and London, are they beyond the line? And is Constantinople the subject of separate judgements? What a difference there is between the overturnings of Catholic and Protestant States! Spain has taken four or five years hard fighting. Holland, the former asylum of the persecuted, is overturned quietly in a day or two. My brother will not imagine that I am dabbling in prophecy—no; all is a mere reverie. Peace and love be with you and yours in our common Lord.

Christ[opher] Anderson

33
Mr. Anderson to Mr. Fuller[1]

December 1, 1813
Edinburgh

We go on progressively at Richmond Court. Our meetings were never better attended. On a Lord's day evening we are occasionally quite crowded. We have our little difficulties, too, but also our pleasures and many blessings. I expect to baptize three persons on my return from Glasgow.[2]

---

[1] Anderson, *Life and Letters*, 96.
[2] Details of the history of this church in Anderson's lifetime is found in Ian L.S. Balfour, *Revival in Rose Street: Charlotte Baptist Chapel, Edinburgh, 1808-2008* (Edinburgh: Rutherford House, 2007), 1-44.

34
Mr. Anderson to Mr. Fuller[1]

July 7, 1814
Liverpool

I have now finished my visit to Ireland,[2] having seen much to interest me there. Another day this people will be known for something eminently good; yet they need to learn something from their neighbours, and by intercourse they will do so. ...

Here, since I began this sheet, have I heard of the death of Brother Sutcliff.[3] It has returned upon me, whether alone or in company. Such an event may well do so. In him I saw bright lines of resemblance to our Lord and Master, such as seldom, very seldom, to be met with in poor mortals. Such amiableness of manners, so much of the meekness and gentleness of Christ, united with sound judgment and warm affection, we seldom or never see united to such a degree as they were in him. While memory holds her place, his name and manner will be cherished by me with a pleasing melancholy; not without anticipation of meeting him another day on the other side of the everlasting hills. What strange, and it may be low ideas of heaven rush into the mind on hearing of the departure of so beloved a man! This morning I thought of him as high in the climes of bliss, met with Pearce;[4] and now while I am writing,

---

[1] Anderson, *Life and Letters*, 224-225.
[2] Information from Anderson's 1814 tour of Ireland and the ongoing interest he showed in Ireland is given in Anderson, *Life and Letters*, 123-124, 134-156.
[3] John Sutcliff died on June 22, 1814.
[4] Samuel Pearce (1766-1999) died in 1799 at the age of 33. He was minister of Canon Street Baptist Church, Birmingham, England, 1790-1799. Andrew Fuller

I have thought of my own father, to whom on earth he was unknown, but who was, in many respects, very like Mr. Sutcliff. So various friends in Scotland have remarked.

Since I came to Liverpool and have heard this, I am the more anxious to see you. I feel to yourself differently from what I did before. On Monday I shall leave this to meet with you, and shall remain as long as I can, consistently with my engagement to be at Edinburgh by Lord's day. Yours very affectionately.

Christ[opher] Anderson

---

compiled the *Memoirs of the late Rev. Samuel Pearce A.M. Minister of the Gospel in Birmingham* (Clipstone: J.W. Morris, 1800). A recent critical edition of this memoir is: Michael A.G. Haykin (ed.), *Memoirs of the Rev. Samuel Pearce* (Boston: De Gruyter, 2017). Reference to the significance of Pearce's ministry is given in a popular account of Baptist witness in the West Midlands. Alan Betteridge, *Deep Roots, Living Branches: A History of Baptists in the English Western Midlands* (Leicester: Matador, 2010), 87–91. See also *The Life of Samuel Pearce* (Peterborough, ON: H&E Publishing, 2020).

35
Mr. Fuller to Mr. Anderson[1]

October 1, 1814
Kettering

Dear friend,

Since I saw you I have had a very serious affliction from which I am not yet recovered, though I am much better and secured by my medical man that I am out of danger. Nearly a month ago I was seized with a bilious attack, and which was followed by a violet inflammation, I suppose in the liver. I had a high fever, was bled and blistered, and for a week confined to my bed, taking calomel medicines. The effects are far from being removed, yet I am much better. On this account you must excuse a short letter, and believe me, &c.

---

[1] Anderson, *Life and Letters*, 226.

36
Mr. Fuller to Mr. Anderson[1]

December 22, 1814
Kettering

Dear brother,

On returning from London last night, I found a letter from Mr. Robert Haldane.[2] He writes in his old strain, and of leaving a pamphlet with you, which I am almost sure I read when last in Scotland, and thought it carried the necessity of a divine revelation so far as to furnish those heathens who have it not with, and not leave them without, excuse.[3]

I have received circular and private letters from Carey and Ward,[4] of as late date as May last. All goes on as well as can be expected. One hundred and sixteen were added in 1813. ...

Our Church affairs are very discouraging. Many disorders in individuals grieve us. Every Church meeting we have things of this kind on hand. My heart is often sinking in me. The Lord undertake for me, and for his own cause! Grace and peace be with you, and yours affectionately,

A. Fuller

---

[1] Anderson, *Life and Letters*, 226.

[2] Robert Haldane (1764-1842) was an evangelical philanthropist and an enthusiastic supporter of many Christian causes, especially home evangelism in Scotland, together with similar work in Switzerland and France. His commitment to theological education and church-planting played a significant role in the establishment of Congregational and Baptist congregations in Scotland. For further details on his life and work, see D.W. Lovegrove, "Haldane, Robert (1764-1842)" in Cameron, ed., *Scottish Church History and Theology*, 386.

[3] Romans 1:20. His important fuller work on this subject was published as: *The Evidence and Authority of Divine Revelation* (2 Vols; Edinburgh: A. Balfour, 1816).

[4] William Carey (1761-1834) and William Ward (1769-1823) were missionaries together in India.

37
Mr. Anderson to Mr. Fuller[1]

December 29, 1814
Edinburgh

My beloved father in Christ Jesus,

For certainly I do feel towards you no small degree of the tenderness and sympathy of a child, however unequal my correspondence may be, I was moved by the latter part of your letter relating to matters at Kettering. The ways of Providence are indeed mysterious, although an explanation to a great degree, is too manifest, too near at hand in many such cases. However, I have noticed in my own limited sphere, that as we must be "tried," if ever we are to be "made white and clean," so God often tries us at home, when he seems to smile upon us abroad; and while public objects in which we have concern are going on well, in our own immediate charge,

> He frowns, and scourges, and rebukes,
> That we may learn His fear.[2]

I am sure I sympathise with you, and that from experience. Before and after my journey to Ireland, we were vexed for months together in this way. But oh! what a refuge have we in

---

[1] Anderson, *Life and Letters*, 226–228.
[2] Philip Doddridge, "The Lord, how kind are all his ways," stanza 1. Philip Doddridge (1702–1751) was a prominent Congregational minister, hymn-writer and theological educator. There are many works written on his life and ministry. The most recent major study is Robert Strivens, *Philip Doddridge and the Shaping of Evangelical Dissent* (London: Taylor and Francis, 2020).

the fellow-feeling of our exalted Lord. I have been struck of late by the consideration of his having taken upon himself, when here below, not only our nature but our condition. And what a passage through life was his! To think of Satan himself setting upon the Son of God, as soon as entered on his public ministry, and pursuing him, by his instruments, throughout the whole course of it! Yet he also felt the weakness of the flesh in hunger and weariness, and wants of almost every description.

It was long before I happened to hear of your last attack; but these repeated afflictions are the occasion of your oft recurring to my mind, I feel so distressed at times about the Mission. You know that my heart and soul have rejoiced in it for years; I cannot, therefore, but feel that its concerns should fall with such undivided pressure on my dear friend. I can be but of little use, especially at this distance, and before I get to the field of action, if the field be England, there is expense involved for travelling.

During the past year I have felt my strength impaired, in a great measure owing to the degree of care and fatigue endured. I long to abridge the former in point of variety, and I expect to be able to do so this spring. For some time past I have been a sort of invalid—pain in my left side has been my chief complaint, and I find I must be cautious. This accounts for delay in regard to the Native Irish, which I have regretted much. Now, however, I am not far from being ready, and mean to send our London friends a proof-sheet or two for their consideration, in the shape of a *Memorial on behalf of the Native Irish*.[3]

---

[3] Christopher Anderson, *Memorial on behalf of the native Irish, with a view to their improvement in moral and religious knowledge through the medium of their own language* (London: Gale, Curtis & Fenner, 1815).

38
Mr. Fuller to Mr. Anderson[1]

January 2, 1815
Kettering

My dear brother,

I duly received both your letters, one of which enclosed a bill of £129, 3s. 3d. Your account is right except the £10 which I first mentioned. ... I had a letter last Friday from Dr. Carey. I find that almost all their revisions and corrections are made during the version's passage through the press; so that the first edition is small, and little more than an experiment. As Carey has fifteen versions now to revise, he has, he says, to read seldom fewer than 120 or 140 pages of proof-sheets in a week, in different languages. ...

I can only add my sympathizing regards under your afflictions. It is soon for you to begin to flag. Grace be with you and your affectionate brother,

A. Fuller

---

[1] Anderson, *Life and Letters*, 228.

39
Mr. Fuller to Mr. Anderson[1]
(the last Mr. Anderson received)

February 18, 1815
Kettering

Dear brother,

I send you a few of the last Memoir of the Translations, with a facsimile of the specimens. If you could make use of them, by presenting them where they would be acceptable and likely to serve the object, I would send by sea five hundred of them in a chest.

One day in conversation with my friend Satchell,[2] he was saying that you and he, when in London, had some talk on the perseverance of believers. He understood you to doubt on that subject. Was it so? And is it a settled point with you? Mr. McLean,[3] in his discourses on the parable of the sower, seems to have some such doubts, and some things which cannot be reconciled with what he has advanced in the "Commission."[4] He there maintains that "all who really believe the gospel are conscious of it, and so have evidence of their own particular salvation." But if believers may apostatize and be lost, a con-

---

[1] Anderson, *Life and Letters*, 228-229.
[2] John Satchell (d.1828). See "Memoir of Mr. John Satchell" in W.T. Brantly, *The Columbian Star and Christian* Index (Philadelphia: Martin & Boden), 1:225-227.
[3] Archibald McLean, leader of the Scotch Baptist connexion in Scotland. "On the Parable of the Sower Matthew 13:18-23," in William Jones, ed., *Works of Mr Archibald McLean* (London: William Jones, 1823), Vol. 4, *Discourses on Various Important Subjects*, 43-83.
[4] Archibald McLean, "The Commission Given by Jesus Christ to His Apostles Illustrated" [originally published 1786] in Jones, ed., *Works of Mr Archibald McLean* (London: William Jones, 1823), 1:1-358.

sciousness of being a believer would afford no such evidence. I have made some remarks on this in my *Letters on Sandemanianism*, pp. 70, 71. Let me hear from you, and tell me your mind on this subject.

I am, your affectionate brother,

A. Fuller

40
Mr. Anderson to Mr. Fuller[1]

March 10, 1815
Edinburgh

My beloved brother,

… I have been greatly obliged and much gratified by your late letters. The beloved Mission, with all its concerns, has as deep a hold on my heart as ever, I hope my endeavours to dispel some of the darkness at home, you will consider as quite compatible with almost daily thoughts of India.

As to our good friend Mr. Satchell's fears, secure him they are groundless. In regard to the subject of final perseverance of the saints of God, as God is possessed of infinite wisdom to devise the plan of redemption, his grace and power are equal to carry it into execution. Oh no; the secret of the Lord is with them that fear him, and he will show them his covenant. If any man be in Christ Jesus, he is a new creature;[2] and the heart being created anew in Christ Jesus, this is assuredly that "which hypocrites could ne'er attain, which false apostates never knew."[3] This, I hope, will satisfy, yet I would add also, that "of all the Father giveth him, he will lose nothing, but will raise up again at the last day."[4] I entirely approve of what you have said in your *Letters*. Perhaps it may have escaped you that I enjoyed the pleasure of talking with you over all the

---

[1] Anderson. *The Life and Letters*, 229-230.
[2] 2 Corinthians 5:17.
[3] Isaac Watts, "The almost Christian, the hypocrite, and apostate," stanza 4.
[4] John 6:39.

subjects of that subjects of that volume, or almost all, either at Kettering, or in journeying together. To return, however, to perseverance. There is, it should seem, no way of discovering apostates but by their apostasy, and consequently the address of a practical, scriptural preacher may seem to militate against the views of some in his auditory. The attainments of apostates, for example, are sufficient, when well described, to make many Christians tremble. What a fine spirit did the Apostles show when our Lord said, "Verily, verily, I say unto you, that one of you shall betray me."[5] And they, each one for himself, trembled and said, "Is it I? Is it I?" I know, however, that brother Satchell subscribes to all this, and I think I see a good man—for I was and am truly attached to him—I see him assenting, Yes, Sir, yes, Sir, very true. But I cannot add the additional remark which he would subjoin; his remarks are so peculiarly his own, ... I am ever, with highest esteem and affection, &c.,

Christ[opher] Anderson

---

[5] Matthew 26:21; John 13:21.

Appendix 1

Mr. Anderson to Dr. Ryland
On the death of Fuller

May 9, 1815
Edinburgh

My esteemed brother,

The first intelligence I had of our present heavy trial, in the affliction of brother Fuller, reached me when in the Highlands; and ever since, all the way home, my heart has been exercised alternately about him and you. Towards both I have felt now for years so much of the feeling of a son and of a brother in Christ Jesus, that whenever there have been threatening appearances at Kettering, Bristol has in my mind been associated with it. And now what shall I say to the letter which I have just received? Grief and sympathy alternately fill my mind, and I feel myself, on this account, but too incompetent to reply. ... Alas! I now fear that all the affection and unfeigned regard which I felt for three is at last about to be transferred to one. Whoever shall be called to engage actively for the Mission, will in your counsel and advice find large support. O may God in mercy spare you to us many years! It would be a balm to my heart to hear from you as soon as possible.

Appendix 2

Anderson on Fuller[1]

We are extremely concerned to record the death of Mr. Andrew Fuller, pastor of the Baptist Church at Kettering, on Lord's day morning, 7th May, in his sixty-second year, and the forty-first of his ministry. Although he was not favoured with a liberal education (which he always regretted), the talents bestowed on him, cultivated with diligence, compensated in a great degree, the want of those advantages which it might have conferred. The singular acuteness and success with which he combated Deism and Socinianism in works very generally read and esteemed, the great variety of his publications on doctrinal, experimental, and practical subjects in religion, his extensive correspondence, and his animated and instructive discourses on his many journeys through different parts of England, Scotland, and Ireland, made him more generally known than most men in the same walk of life. The richness of his invention, the depth of his knowledge in the Scriptures, and his eminent usefulness, were open to all. But those alone who intimately knew the warmth, frankness, and sincerity of his heart, can rightly appreciate the loss sustained by his family, his friends, the church he served, and the other churches which looked up to him for advice and assistance. Above all, the Mission in India, originating with him and a few

---

[1] This was understood to be from Anderson and appeared in an unidentified Edinburgh periodical on May 12, 1815. See Anderson, *Life and Letters*, 231–232.

other friends, fostered and extended through the extraordinary blessing of heaven, by their indefatigable care, will have cause, it is feared, to deplore the loss of zeal, wisdom, and influence, devoted with assiduity and success to its interests. It is to be hoped that his much lamented death will be considered by many as a new and urgent call to abound still more in liberality towards that most important object to which his distinguished abilities were so actively devoted for two and twenty years.

Appendix 3

Mr. Fuller to Mr. Ward, Serampore, India[1]

December 10, 1807
Kettering

There are two excellent men in Scotland among the Baptists,[2] Christopher Anderson, who was with Brother Sutcliffe a while, and is now trying to raise a Baptist Church in Edinburgh, not from other denominations, but out of Satan's kingdom. I believe God will bless that man. If I dare try to remove him from Edinburgh, and could induce him to come and be co-pastor with me, I would divide my income with him; and he would take my place in the Mission, if he survived me; and he is not twenty-five years old. He is a fine writer, a close thinker, a good preacher; and what is more, a holy, diligent, mild character. Indeed, should anything turn out for his leaving Edinburgh, I know he would be caught at by the first Churches of our denomination. Mr. Booth's[3] Church would have had him, but his heart was so set on Edinburgh, that he would not hear a word of it. Yet he has no church there at

---

[1] Anderson, *The Life and Letters*, 182-183.
[2] The other man he was thinking of was George Barclay of Irvine. See Talbot, *Search for a Common Identity*, 127-144.
[3] Abraham Booth (1734-1806). Anderson was invited three times by Prescott church, while he was studying at Bristol. See Anderson, *Life and Letters*, 50,54-55,418. An excellent brief account of the life and work of Booth is Robert Oliver, "Abraham Booth (1734-1806)," in Michael A.G. Haykin (ed.) *British Particular Baptists 1638-1910* (Springfield, MI: Particular Baptist Press, 2000), 2:30-55.

present, nor one right-hand friend who stands by him, nor does he receive anything at present for his labours. I should not think it lawful to invite him to Kettering, while so many other stations are unoccupied, but for the sake of training him up to take my place in the Mission. Whether he will move I cannot tell yet. He is not skilled, I believe, in languages. Our people are delighted with him. If they could have him, and I were not too old, I might come and join you.

Appendix 4

Mr. Fuller to Mr. Marshman, Serampore[1]

May 15, 1812
Kettering

... I have written to Christopher Anderson of Edinburgh, proposing to his serious consideration his leaving his station, and his coming to succeed me as the pastor of Kettering Church, and Secretary to the Mission. I have had much said to me of late on the subject, and have thought much of it myself. There is no man in Britain whose heart is more in the work, who is readier address, and but few of more acceptable talents, and who has so ready a use of the pen. He might, while I live, come and help me, and when I die, if he survive, succeed me.

He must be about thirty years of age. I have not received an answer.

---

[1] Anderson, *Life and Letters*, 207.

Appendix 5

Mr. Fuller to Mr. Ward, Serampore[1]

July 9, 1812
Derby

... When at Bristol I received an anonymous letter from London. The handwriting was that of Joseph Gutteridge[2] — expressing the satisfaction that generally prevailed respecting the conduct of the Mission, and that there could be no wish to take it out of the hands it was in; but inquiring whether provision were made for its security, in case of those who at present conducted it being removed or laid aside; proposing also that there should be Corresponding Committee chosen in London, Edinburgh, Bristol, &c. Upon the whole it was a friendly letter, and I thanked him for it, assuring him that the subject was under consideration. I have since conversed much with friends upon a future plan. The probability on the above plan would be, that though during the lifetime of a few of us we should naturally have the direction, it would afterwards go into the hands of some of those committees. Some said, "If you have a committee at London, have others at Bristol, Ed-

---

[1] Anderson, *Life and Letters*, 207-209.

[2] Joseph Gutteridge was a deacon of the Prescott Street Baptist Church where Abraham Booth was minister in London. For more details on his life and especially his involvement in the management of the Baptist Missionary Society, see E. Steane, *Memoir of the Life of Joseph Gutteridge, Esq* (London: Jackson and Walford, Partridge and Oakey, 1850), 110-122.

inburgh, &c, as a balance against them; for, if it goes to London, it goes to a vortex of vanity." Another (C[hristopher] A[nderson]) said,

> I know what committees are—many men, many minds, and, after all, one or two direct. You had better choose that one or two without their appendages. A body of men feel themselves of consequence, and will do something to signalize themselves, though it be in opposition to the rest. My advice is, let the committee be one and indivisible—enlarge it by adding to it those active ministers through kingdom, whose hearts are already in it. They cannot unite with you in consultation, for local reasons; but they can and will serve the object, and when you die, or are laid aside, some one of them, either in your place, or at the post he may be in, will be the Secretary in your stead. Let there be a few brethren from London among them, but let the seat of the Society be where it is, in your own *Association*. There it originated, and there it had best continue.

Such are the outlines of a plan that I have drawn up to be considered at the Kettering Ministers' Meeting, 29th September, of which you will have the result. I know of but two of our ministers that could succeed me. *First*, Christopher Anderson of Edinburgh. He could do it. He could do almost anything that I do, and some things better. I have accordingly consulted with my brethren, and invited him to come, and be my fellow-labourer at Kettering, and put on the yoke. His heart is deeply in the Mission. He is popular as a preacher, clever with his pen, under thirty years of age, affable, ingratiating, preserving, affectionate. He was overcome with the request, but could not give me an answer; said he must see me. I accord-

Appendix

ingly met him; we were nearly two days together. The result was:

> I have my head, hands, and heart full already with the Secretaryship of Edinburgh Bible Society, and the Gaelic Schools, and the pastorship of the Church, raised up in the last few years under my own ministry—I cannot possibly stir at present—I hope you will live some years yet. Choose me as one of your committee, and I will do all I can for you. I will also throw off my other engagements as I can get others to take them off my hands, and in two or three years we shall see what will take place. He spent a month in Liverpool this summer, and set on foot a Society for the Translations, which has already sent me £146 amidst all the commercial distress of that town. But he is attached to a city life, which is against his coming hither. ...

Appendix 6

Mr. Fuller to Mr. Ward, Serampore[1]

November 17, 1812

... I wish you to be better acquainted with Christopher Anderson of Edinburgh, and send him a set of circular letters. He is the only man in Britain who promises to conduct the Mission as Secretary, should I die; but I may yet live for years.

---

[1] Anderson, *Life and Letters*, 235.

Appendix 7

John Satchell to Mr. Anderson[1]

On Friday I desired Mr. Fuller to have the goodness to leave some expression of his wishes with respect to his successor, as I knew it would have very great weight with the church; on Monday, 1st May, at half-past three, p.m., he sent for Mr. Collier (a deacon) and myself to his bedside. I put the question, and he answered in exactly the following words, the last I ever heard him speak: "I know of no one who would do the church so much good as Mr. Anderson of Edinburgh." The uttering of these words quite spent him, and we immediately took our leave.

---

[1] Anderson, *Life and Letters*, 235.

Index

A

Anderson, William, 1
Antinomianism, 17
Apostasy, 58, 120

B

Baptism, 1, 25, 33, 38, 47, 69
Baptist Irish Society, 29, 31, 59
Baptist Magazine, 5, 13, 29, 33, 49, 59, 63
Baptist Missionary Society, 1, 2, 3, 5, 6, 10, 13, 15, 19, 23, 27, 28, 35, 37, 38, 47, 49, 51, 59, 81, 83, 84, 87, 91, 93, 95, 129
Barclay, George, 3, 29, 31, 76, 125
Bengal, 47, 81, 84, 93
Bible Society, 3, 5, 13, 33, 47, 51, 60, 65, 76, 82, 85, 131
Booth, Abraham, 125, 129
Bristol Baptist College, 63
Bunyan, John, 17
Burditt, J., 49
Burls, William, 49, 62, 67, 97
Burnett, John, 82

C

Campbell, George, 62
Campbell, John, 94
Carey, William, 14, 35, 38, 47, 68, 83, 94, 111, 115
Charles, Thomas, 76
Charlotte Chapel, 3
Chundra, Deep, 38
Coles, Ann, 11, 43
Constantinople, 103, 104
Cowper, William, 32

D

Dass, Kristna, 84
Deakin, James, 91
Discouragement, 21, 77, 81
Doddridge, Philip, 113
Dublin, 34

E

East India Company, 93, 94
Edinburgh, ix, 1, 2, 3, 7, 9, 10, 15, 17, 19, 23, 28, 31, 32, 37, 39, 47, 54, 57, 59, 62, 71, 72, 75, 76, 77, 81, 82, 87, 91, 93, 94, 97, 99, 103, 105, 108, 111, 113, 119, 121, 123, 125, 127, 129, 130, 131, 133, 135
Edinburgh Review, 31, 32
Egypt, 103
Evangelical Magazine, 6, 60, 72
Ewing, Greville, 28, 97

F

Friendship, 4, 6, 9, 10, 12, 13, 14, 35, 37, 39, 48, 53, 54, 57, 62, 63, 85, 91, 93, 109, 114, 117, 119, 126
Fuller, Joseph, 33, 69
Fuller, Sarah, 43

G

Gaelic School Society, 3, 76
Gardiner, Sarah, 11, 43
Glasgow, 76, 91, 97, 105
Gutteridge, Joseph, 129

H

Haldane, Alexander, 28
Haldane, James, 1, 28
Haldane, Robert, 111
Hall Jr., Robert, 29, 31, 69, 88, 99, 102
Hall, John, 69
Harington, John Herbert, 85
Heaven, 8, 21, 66, 87, 92, 107, 124
Hill, Rowland, 65
Hinton, James, 60, 63, 67
Holland, 104
Holy Spirit, 21, 89
Hughes, Joseph, 60, 64

I

Income, 10, 15, 27, 125
India, 2, 19, 23, 37, 47, 49, 67, 68, 87, 94, 101, 111, 119, 123, 125
Inverness, 76, 97, 99
Ireland, 3, 29, 31, 34, 76, 97, 107, 113, 123
Irish Baptists, 34
Ivimey, Joseph, 59, 60, 97

J

Jelburgh, 99
John, Griffith, 76
Judaism, 54

K

Kelso, 99
Kettering, 3, 14, 15, 23, 24, 27, 33, 43, 49, 51, 53, 54, 59, 67, 68, 69, 77, 79, 83, 88, 89, 94, 95, 97, 101, 109, 111, 113, 115, 117, 120, 121, 123, 125, 126, 127, 130

King, Thomas, 51

L

Lisbon, 104
Liverpool, 7, 59, 63, 65, 107, 108, 131
London, 1, 2, 5, 14, 17, 18, 23, 24, 28, 29, 38, 47, 48, 49, 54, 55, 57, 59, 60, 62, 63, 65, 83, 84, 85, 97, 101, 103, 111, 113, 114, 117, 129, 130
London Missionary Society, 65
Lord's Supper, 20, 28

M

MacKnight, James, 62
Madrid, 104
Mahometanism, 54
Mardon, Richard, 84
Marischal College, 62
Marshman, Joshua, 47, 81, 83, 127
McLean, Archibald, 17, 18, 28, 59, 117
Miscarriage, 11, 43
Morris, John Webster, 28, 35, 53, 58, 59
Moscow, 103
Moubray, Jean, 1
Mulberry tree, 21, 23

N

Newman, William, 60
Newton, John, 57
Norfolk, 35, 83
Norwich, 83

P

Paganism, 54
Palestine, 103

Index

Patient, Thomas, 34
Pearce, Samuel, 2, 8, 34, 51, 66, 107, 108
Peebles, 99
Periodical Accounts, 13, 37, 47, 49, 83, 89
Plurality of elders, 27
Popery, 54
Prayer, 40, 68, 72
Preaching, 1, 3, 6, 10, 17, 20, 23, 29, 37, 65, 72, 75, 89, 93

R

Richmond Court, 2, 27, 77, 81, 105
Roman Catholicism, 61, 104
Rowe, Joshua, 38
Russia, 104
Ryland Jr., John, 5, 17, 33, 35, 63, 79, 121
Ryland, John Collett, 63

S

Saffery, John, 29
Satchell, John, 117, 135
Scotch Baptists, 17, 38
Scotch Itinerant Society, 76
Scotland, ix, 1, 2, 3, 5, 17, 19, 23, 27, 28, 29, 32, 62, 68, 76, 91, 94, 95, 97, 99, 101, 108, 111, 117, 123, 125

Selkirk, 99
Serampore fire, 83
Smith, William, 79
Soham, 23
Spain, 104
Steadman, William, 33
Stepney Academy, 60
Stewart, Alexander, 97
Stockholm, 103, 104
Stuart, Charles, 28, 48, 59, 82, 89, 91, 93, 99, 101
Sunday Schools, 65
Sutcliff, John, 2, 7, 28, 35, 62, 67, 99, 107, 108
Sutcliffe, John, 125
Swam, Thomas, 14

T

Turnbull, William, 14

U

Usefulness, 2, 5, 14, 17, 20, 23, 24, 25, 123

W

Ward, William, 10, 47, 83, 111, 125, 133
Watts, Isaac, 103, 119
Wilks, Mark, 83

www.ingramcontent.com/pod-product-compliance
Lightning Source LLC
Chambersburg PA
CBHW021111080526
44587CB00010B/472